Jennifer Saake

D1008119

hannah's
hope

Seeking
God's Heart
in the
Midst of
Infertility

NAVPRESS®

BRINGING TRUTH TO LIFE

OUR GUARANTEE TO YOU

We believe so strongly in the message of our books that we are making this quality guarantee to you. If for any reason you are disappointed with the content of this book, return the title page to us with your name and address and we will refund to you the list price of the book. To help us serve you better, please briefly describe why you were disappointed. Mail your refund request to: NavPress, P.O. Box 35002, Colorado Springs, CO 80935.

The Navigators is an international Christian organization. Our mission is to reach, disciple, and equip people to know Christ and to make Him known through successive generations. We envision multitudes of diverse people in the United States and every other nation who have a passionate love for Christ, live a lifestyle of sharing Christ's love, and multiply spiritual laborers among those without Christ.

NavPress is the publishing ministry of The Navigators. NavPress publications help believers learn biblical truth and apply what they learn to their lives and ministries. Our mission is to stimulate spiritual formation among our readers.

ISBN 1-57683-654-1

Cover design by Studiogearbox.com
Cover photo by Photonica
Creative Team: Rachelle Gardner, Amy Spencer, Darla Hightower, Arvid Wallen, Glynese Northam

Some of the anecdotal illustrations in this book are true to life and are included with the permission of the persons involved. All other illustrations are composites of real situations, and any resemblance to people living or dead is coincidental.

Portions of this work have been adapted from articles author has published 1995–2003 at www.hannah. org and/or 1995-2004 in "Hannah to Hannah," the newsletter of Hannah's Prayer Ministries, PO Box 168, Hanford, CA 93232-0168.

Some tips in Burden Bearers sections have been adapted from "What Your Infertile/Bereaved Friend Would Like You to Know but Doesn't Know How to Tell You Herself," copyright © 2003 by Jennifer Saake, from the *Hannah's Prayer Ministries Favorite Recipes* cookbook.

Unless otherwise identified, all Scripture quotations in this publication are taken from the HOLY BIBLE: NEW INTERNATIONAL VERSION® (NIV®). Copyright © 1973, 1978, 1984 by International Bible Society. Used by permission of Zondervan Publishing House. All rights reserved. *The King James Version* (KJV) is also quoted.

Saake, Jennifer, 1972-
Hannah's hope : seeking God's heart in the midst of infertility, miscarriage, and adoption loss / Jennifer Saake.-- 1st ed.
    p. cm.
Includes bibliographical references.
ISBN 1-57683-654-1
1. Hannah (Biblical figure) 2. Bible. O.T. Samuel, 1st I-II--Criticism, interpretation, etc. 3. Childlessness in the Bible. 4. Miscarriage--Religious aspects--Christianity. 5. Adoption--Religious aspects--Christianity. I. Title.
BS1325.52.S23 2005
248.8'6--dc22
                2005002529

Printed in the United States of America

2 3 4 5 6 7 8 9 10 / 08 07 06

FOR A FREE CATALOG OF
NAVPRESS BOOKS & BIBLE STUDIES,
CALL 1-800-366-7788 (USA)
OR 1-800-839-4769 (CANADA)

"Jennifer is candid and transparent, standing beside us in our barrenness — the one thing that every heartbroken parent needs instead of platitudes that simply fall on the dry ground of our souls. We heartily recommend this resource for every parent whose arms may be empty but who hold their precious children forever in their hearts."

— RUSS AND JUNE GORDON
founders, A Quiet Refuge, a pregnancy and infant loss ministry;
authors of *Forever in Our Hearts*

"*Hannah's Hope* is for all who have felt alone on the path of infertility, pregnancy loss, or failed adoption. Readers gain two worthy companions — author Jennifer Saake and the biblical character Hannah. This wisdom-filled guide to the marital, emotional, and spiritual crisis of empty arms is a terrific resource for both those who ache and those who love them."

— SANDRA GLAHN
adjunct professor, Dallas Theological Seminary;
author, *When Empty Arms Become a Heavy Burden* and *The Infertility Companion*

"This compassionate and candid book will surely serve as a balm to the hearts of those who find themselves crushed and bewildered by the pain of infertility, miscarriage, or failed adoption."

— JANET EASON
president, Georgia Chapter of Resolve;
infertility survivor and adoptive mother of Ellie

"This book is so compassionately and honestly written! Jennifer Saake writes candidly, addressing multiple issues of infertility, miscarriage, and adoption loss. I can see how God will use this talented, heartfelt writer to help people through the pain of infertility, miscarriage, and adoption loss."

— LISA WITTS
R.N.

"Both practical and profound, *Hannah's Hope* is an honest, compelling look at the spiritually and physically challenging issue of infertility. It will prove immeasurably helpful to the onlooker as well as to those personally encountering the challenges. *Hannah's Hope* goes beyond the infertility issues to core spiritual principles we all need to embrace, whatever the source of our pain."

— MARTHA L. KELFER
president, Discipleship Tape Ministries, Inc.

"*Hannah's Hope* is by far the best book I have read on infertility and loss. Jennifer openly shares her personal struggles, such as how her faith is tested as everyone around her seems to obtain the honor of motherhood effortlessly. Each chapter ends with a section called "Burden Bearers," in which Jennifer provides immeasurable guidance on how our friends and family can best minister to us as we seek God for His perfect, ultimate, and individual plan for our lives."

— KIM CONGER
general director, Hannah's Prayer Ministries

"What a great tool to add to a pastor's tool box — powerful and practical. I especially appreciate the scholarly treatment of Hannah that is woven into Jennifer and Rick's painful story."
— KEVIN WOOD
pastor

"Through her heartache and longing for a child, Jennifer is sure to reach many readers on a level that they only wish others could understand. Whether you are struggling with infertility yourself or just a supporter of someone who is going through this difficult time, Jennifer is sure to give you accurate information on infertility and, most important, touch your soul."
— NICKI WRIGHT
volunteer chairperson, Resolve of Ohio

"Just as there is no deeper love than that of parents for their child, there is no grief more intense than the heartache experienced by parents who never get to hold their baby. It's an anguish that Jennifer Saake knows all too well. Rather than allowing her pain to immobilize her, however, Jennifer has bravely allowed God to use her to minister to others walking this lonely road — including my wife and me. *Hannah's Hope* is a gift from God to every family who longs for a child they may never see this side of heaven."
— GLEN HOOS
director of resource development, FamilyLife Canada

"As a previous mom-in-waiting, I wish Saake's book was available when I was experiencing the roller-coaster ride of infertility. *Hannah's Hope* reflects the emotions of my journey, most especially that which I was too embarrassed to admit — like skipping church on Mother's Day! This book will bring comfort and understanding to women, their spouses, and even their loved ones. God faithfully provides comfort through Saake's willingness to share her own vulnerabilities of grief and, of course, hope."
— LISA COPEN
director, Rest Ministries; editor, HopeKeepers magazine

"What a deeply personal and instructive book! This is a must-read for anyone ministering in the body of Christ. Jennifer Saake opens her heart and our eyes to the needs of couples struggling with infertility. Her compassionate style and scripturally based approach brings hope to hurting hearts and wisdom to those who desire to be supportive companions on the journey."
— JAN FRANK
M.F.T., coauthor of *Unclaimed Baggage* and *Door of Hope*

"This book is a must-read for all the women who have or are going through infertility problems. It speaks of a journey that turns your mourning into dancing and your sorrows into joy. You realize that you're not alone and that hope, faith, and a life of worship leads us all to our miracle. It did for me! I pray that this book will bring a great blessing, breakthrough, and revelation of God's love, purpose, and promises to everyone who reads it."
— DONIA MAKEDONEZ
singer and songwriter, Hillsong Church, Australia

For Rick, who knows my heart and lovingly encourages my dreams. Thank you for loving the Lord first, then giving me second place, above all others.

contents

acknowledgments

Many, many people have been instrumental in the creation of *Hannah's Hope*:

This book would not exist without the grace of the Lord Jesus Christ. Studying Hannah's life has given me a new appreciation of the price He paid for my redemption and of the amazing freedom I have in Him, apart from the regulations of the Old Testament Law. Lord, thank you for not abandoning me, even when I doubted your love.

Hannah. How I look forward to meeting her in heaven! Thank you, Hannah, for being an example of grace in the midst of grief.

My husband, Rick, who believed in and encouraged my writing from the beginning, who pushed me out of my comfort zone to learn computers and the Internet, and who humored me as God took our small, local support group and blossomed it into an international ministry. Rick has stood by me through much "better and worse" and has taken up the slack around home during the writing of this book. Thank you, Rick, for digging through Laundry Mountain every morning without complaint.

Joshua and Ruth, my precious miracle blessings. Thank you for sharing your mommy with the computer, the writing of this book, and thousands of "Hannah's Prayer Mommies who are sad because they don't have their babies yet/anymore."

Dad (Ralph Camp), for footsteps pacing above his office, countless phone calls, allowing himself to be sucked into my projects, listening and being a wise sounding board as I've battled my way through this journey of faith. Thank you, Dad, for making my passions a priority in your own heart.

Mom (Betty), for countless hours as my homeschool teacher, showing this dyslexic girl how to embrace the written word. Thank you for your precious friendship and prayers.

Grandma Dorothy, for opening up the world of writing. Give my babies a big hug for me today in heaven.

Debra Bridwell, my mentor. Thank you for letting God use your vulnerability to change my life in such a profound way.

Julie Donahue, founder of Ladies In Waiting. What history we share! Thank you (and John) for not giving up when ministry was rough.

Kathe Wunnenberg, for helping me "grieve the children I never knew" and challenging me to put action behind my dreams. This book would still be a "someday" goal without you.

All past and present members of the Hannah's Prayer board of directors and honorary board, Dad, Debra, Kathe, Julie, Leslie Snodgrass, Sandra Glahn, Diane (Benedict) Dickinson, Stephanie Bixler (general director 2001–2002), Kim Conger (current general director), Nancy Hill, Kim Joslin, David Davis, Kate Anderson. Thank you for your wisdom, leadership, and great dedication to comforting thousands of hurting hearts with the comfort you have received in Christ.

Hannah's Prayer Ministries members. Thank you for sharing your hearts and lives. Special thanks to all who allowed me to share portions of your stories within these pages: Tina, Jane, Steve and Nancy, Glen and Christie, Joanie, Katie Jane, Beth, Alison, Brad and Jennifer Ballard, Stephanie Brandt, Janelle Dressen, Kelley Eck, Denise England, Heather Hester, Pamela Houghton, Ruth Leamy, Tracey Pettijohn, Scott and Michele Pickle, Nicolle Reece Jan Sanders, Raegan Sasser, and Miriam Wrye.

My worldwide prayer partners including my parents-in-love — Norm and Patty Saake, the JennisWriting e-mail list, the Rest Ministries Venture Quencher gang, the "Writer's Heart" Women of Faith, and my phone-call-away friend, Sue. Thank you for the tremendous support each time I shared prayer needs, both minor and urgent.

Ladies of Reno Christian Fellowship's Thursday morning Bible study. Thank you for your prayers, encouragement, and sharpening iron.

Lisa Witts. Thank you for your loving care of my children, providing the hours I needed to make this book a reality. Your fresh reminders about "living the wait" helped fill these pages.

Martha Kelfer. Thank you for the glimpses into Russell's heart and your own.

Jan Frank. Thank you for teaching me much about "waiting gracefully" and for pointing me to the publisher God had for this project.

Everyone at NavPress, especially Rachelle Gardner and the entire creative team, Nicci Jordan, and Trina Miller. Thank you for believing the topics of infertility, miscarriage, and adoption loss are important enough to take a risk with this new author, and for all your assistance through the process.

introduction

The LORD is my shepherd, I shall not be in want. He makes me
lie down in green pastures, he leads me beside quiet waters, he
restores my soul. He guides me in paths of righteousness for
his name's sake. Even though I walk through the valley of the
shadow of death, I will fear no evil, for you are with me; your
rod and your staff, they comfort me.

PSALM 23:1-4

Two roads diverged in a wood, and I—
I took the one less traveled by,
And that has made all the difference.

ROBERT FROST

Allow me to introduce you to my dear friend Hannah, whom I've never
met. How did I come to call Hannah my friend without even meeting her?
She is my companion because we share a common heartbeat. Hannah's heart
pounded with a mother's love long before she was blessed with a child to
mother. Through the years of waiting and longing, her gentle heart was nearly
crushed under the weight of grief. Find her story recorded in 1 Samuel 1–2.

In today's terminology, we would say that Hannah was either *infertile*
(unable to conceive within one year of regular marital relations without
the use of birth control, or unable to carry a child to live birth) or *sterile*
(permanently unable to produce the genetic materials required to conceive
a child). By simply describing Hannah as *barren,* the Bible does not give us
many specific details about her medical condition. What we do know is that

Hannah suffered heartache, anguish, and grief because of her empty arms. Are you a "Hannah" too?

If motherhood is your goal and you are disillusioned in trying to reach this destination, keep reading! This book is written for every family that longs for a child yet-to-be-conceived, that grieves for a baby too-soon-passed from the womb into heaven, or that has lived through the no-man's-land of failed adoption. It is intended as a guide to assist you in decisions as you struggle through grief. By the end of this journey, God may surprise you by the methods He uses to answer your heart's cry.

Or perhaps you are a "Burden Bearer" for a loved one on such an odyssey. If you are a pastor, friend, or family member who desires to help someone else through this valley, I offer my most sincere gratitude for your compassion, and I will offer suggestions to you.

When yearning for motherhood, years become measured in months and cycles. Of the first eleven years of my marriage (that's over 140 chances for pregnancy if counting twenty-eight-day cycles), more than ten years were spent actively striving to grow our family. If my husband, Rick, and I weren't aggressively trying to conceive or longingly seeking to adopt, we were anxiously praying to sustain troubled pregnancies and grieving our many losses along the way. What a long, weary journey it has been.

I must admit to finishing this book "from the other side" of the infertility expedition, now with two living blessings to fill our lives with all the laughter, dirty fingerprints, scattered toys, and bedtime hugs we so longed for. But before you stop reading and walk away, feeling me to be disqualified to address this tender topic, please know that this book has been actively in the writing process for many years.

Much of what I share on these pages is pulled directly from my private journals, recording all the anger, grief, longing, isolation, questions, struggles, tears, sorrows — and even joy — relief, excitement, and answered prayers along the way.

While we are now parents, it was a life-altering battle that led us here. Hormonal imbalances, reproductive abnormalities, immune system dysfunction, and the desire for a larger family remain our realities. As founder of a ministry called Hannah's Prayer, I have learned much from thousands of amazing families who have trusted me with their pain as they have grieved for children. Am I qualified to guide you on this exploration of Hannah's heart? I pray that you will find it to be so.

While it was indeed a road less traveled, this winding way of childlessness was one I did not *choose* to tread. I often limped along this uphill trail, kicking and fighting my way through the dense underbrush of discouragement. But through the journey, God provided green pastures where my aching soul could draw comfort from the recognition that my loving heavenly Father approved the course before allowing me to take my first step.

When I first met Hannah, I defined myself exclusively as *infertile*, leading a barren life, without hope. With my course on this less-frequented path plotted against my will, there was one fork in the road that did require my decision: Would I choose bitterness and self-destruction, or growth and renewed hope? The seemingly easier path was anger with God, but I needed to choose the trail that would truly make all the difference. In slowly finding kinship with Hannah, I have realized that my fertility challenges need not destroy me. Intense anger and bitterness have been replaced by a peace that comes only from God.

I want to bring the historical account of Hannah's life alive for you, as it has been for me. Each chapter begins with a brief fictionalized look at a portion of Hannah's story. I've taken the liberty of imagining some of the details of Hannah's infertility journey, basing them on the historical context in which she lived and on my own experience with barrenness. While reflecting on Hannah's heart I will also share pieces of my story, along with the stories of other families facing fertility challenges.

Through all of this I've found that, when I shift my focus from my human *in*abilities and infertility and seek God's strength to surmount fertility challenges according to His guidance, hope is rekindled. In getting to know this woman of old, I pray that the reflections of Hannah's heart will direct you to the Source of her strength, whose name is the God of All Comfort.

my story

Since early childhood, I had imagined I would grow up to raise eight kids! Our August 1992 wedding was quickly followed by the active pursuit of parenthood. By then, Rick and I dreamed of "at least four," through birth, adoption, or both, however God might provide.

In April 1994, we hadn't become pregnant yet, but received our first serious adoption lead. For thirty-six joyful hours we prepared our hearts and home for the preschool-aged son and daughter we believed could soon be joining us. But God had another family planned for these children, and we had to let them go.

After two years of medical fertility assistance, we stepped back from treatments in October of 1994, having exhausted our insurance, finances, and emotional reserves. We refocused our energies and began forming *Hannah's Prayer Ministries*, a Christian infertility support network. Though I rarely ovulated even on fertility drugs, my body experienced a "rebound" reaction to the cessation of monthly rounds of Clomid. To our surprise, we conceived our first biological child in early December. Noel was miscarried December 26/27.

God brought many adoption possibilities into our lives over the following years. Sometimes we easily saw that leads wouldn't work out. But we believed parenthood to be imminent with each of five more children, only to reap shattered hope and empty arms at the end of each encounter.

A young woman with a history of past abortions was able to carry her baby to live birth in 1995 because she knew adoption was an option. Just weeks before birth, we learned of her ultimate decision to parent her daughter.

In 1996, God called us to a painful season of supporting a friend through a pregnancy that would eventually allow her to place her son in the arms of another family. After the emotional drain of that experience, we stepped back from any adoption attempts for the next couple years.

We dabbled in fertility treatments again, but didn't have the financial resources to pursue the aggressive treatments doctors recommended. By now several medical conditions that inhibited our fertility were also significantly impacting my overall health. I underwent my first surgery for endometriosis (where we discovered my uterine deformity, a bicornate or "heart-shaped" uterus that can cause pregnancy complications and loss). About this time, I also found a doctor who was willing to prescribe groundbreaking medication to address my PCOS (polycystic ovarian syndrome), failure to ovulate, acne, excess weight gain, and overall health decline, by dealing with underlying issues of insulin resistance.

In January of 1999, we learned of a young mother in the next state, in labor at that very moment, wanting to meet us. I had been ready to pursue adoption again for quite a while, but this was the first time Rick shared my desire after the scars of previous losses. Hope sprung as we packed our bags to meet our daughter. But the next phone call never came.

A few months later, a single woman I had previously supported through high-risk pregnancy and infant death called to explain that she was again pregnant and would like us to adopt her new baby. Soon thereafter she learned "the baby" was *twins*! As I'd prayed specifically for twins since I was only three years old, this seemed like a dream come true! Our dream shattered the moment her state's social services brought to light her history of mental illness and ongoing adoption scams. She had never been pregnant, even when I had previously supported her during "pregnancy complications" and "infant death." At the same time she was telling us we were the "only family" right for her children, she was leading along at least five other families in as many states.

I felt used, angry, hurt, lonely, and lost in a sea of grief. We had been praying to grow our family for six and a half years and faced the "deaths" (emotional or physical) of our first eight children!

Through a series of God-ordained circumstances, we headed into higher levels of fertility treatment and began injecting my body full of hormones. Three IUI cycles later, we received the phone call of our lives — a positive pregnancy test! While my initial hormone levels were excellent (even indicating the possibility of multiples), pregnancy got off to a rocky start with early bleeding and cramping. It was a bittersweet relief to find one, but only one, beautiful heartbeat on the ultrasound screen.

I struggled with severe "morning sickness" the entire pregnancy, only gaining a net total of six pounds. By the Lord's exceeding grace, Joshua was born on December 22, 1999, full term and healthy, but weighing under five pounds. It took three more pregnancies before we learned the reason for his low birth weight was not due to my lack of weight gain, but caused by an immunity issue that, untreated, results in an 80-89 percent gestational mortality rate.

Since it had taken so long the first time, we didn't take any break from trying to conceive after Joshua's birth. This time it only took a year to conceive, using over-the-counter progesterone supplements but no other infertility interventions. However, Joel's miscarriage began about three days after we realized I was pregnant. LPD (Luteal Phase Defect, a shortened post-ovulation phase of the monthly cycle and progesterone levels insufficient to sustain pregnancy) was the diagnosed cause of his death.

I started monthly prescription progesterone treatment and was shocked by another positive pregnancy test just three months later. This baby shared Joshua's due date from two years prior, the exact timing I had hoped for between children! When bleeding started two days later, my progesterone dosage was increased, but not in time to save Hannah's life.

More than a year passed without another conception, and the Lord began to soften our hearts toward adoption yet again. We felt led to investigate international adoption and were in the early stages of working with an agency to find a daughter in China. When other two-year-olds were watching *Blue's Clues* and *Thomas the Tank Engine*, Joshua's favorite was our orientation video with all the faces of children in Chinese orphanages.

In January 2002 I landed back in the operating room for what was expected to be a simple, forty-five-minute laparoscopy to remove mild endometriosis. Instead, during the three-and-a-half-hour procedure, my doctor found severe adhesions and asked Rick to allow him to remove a tube and ovary. Rick refused to make that decision without me, so I came out of anesthesia to learn that I would have to return to surgery within the next three to six months, probably three.

I now had less than a 5 percent chance of ever again conceiving. I received this startling news with uncommon peace. With at least three of our biological children in heaven rather than on earth, pregnancy was a fearful prospect. Though I grieved that I might never carry another child, it was a relief to think that the struggle and month-to-month wondering would soon be behind us. My heart was already in China, and I was willing for my body to be done with this long journey.

When I wasn't feeling well a couple weeks before my next surgery date, I attributed it to my recent stop in progesterone supplementation. I took a pregnancy test on a whim and actually threw it away, thinking it defective, when a second line popped up! But God had done what doctors could not do. With only minor medical intervention, we were expecting the child who statistically should never have been conceived nor carried.

Early testing revealed my elevated IgM levels, the factor we now believe to have caused IUGR (inter-uterine growth retardation) for Joshua. I took blood thinners on a daily basis for the rest of the pregnancy, accompanied by monthly ultrasound growth checks. Pre-term contractions caught us by unhappy surprise in my twenty-fifth week. I was put on a combination of activity restrictions and bed rest for the next thirteen weeks, along with medication to arrest labor as the pregnancy progressed. Ruth weighed in at nearly six and a half pounds when she was born on January 25, 2003.

After twelve years and with two living children, is our family complete? We honestly don't know. For the first time in our married lives, we are no longer actively seeking to grow our family, yet we are open to God's will if His plan is otherwise. Expecting that childbearing will only grow continually harder for my body, we aren't planning on any more biological children (but then, we weren't expecting to conceive Ruth either). Adoption still holds a tender spot in our hearts, and we wonder if God may yet lead us back down this path sometime in the future.

family ties

There was a certain man from Ramathaim, a Zuphite from the hill country of Ephraim, whose name was Elkanah son of Jeroham, the son of Elihu, the son of Tohu, the son of Zuph, an Ephraimite.

1 SAMUEL 1:1

So God created man in his own image, in the image of God he created him; male and female he created them. . . . God saw all that he had made, and it was very good.

GENESIS 1:27, 31

Hannah had been nervous to meet her betrothed, unsure of this man with whom she was to share her life. But her family had chosen well. To Hannah's delight, Elkanah proved to be a godly man whom she was quickly learning to love.

A gentle blush crept over her face as she thought of the words of blessing confidently shouted by merrymakers on their recent wedding day: 'May your descendants be like the sands on the seashore and the stars in the sky. May you be fruitful like Rachel and Leah, who together built up the house of Israel.' Hannah dreamily pictured herself holding Elkanah's son in her arms by the following year. And if not yet in her arms, then surely within her womb.

But that first year passed, then another, then yet another. Discouragement, grief, and fear silently stole away innocent hope. To avoid looks of pity, she lowered her eyes each time she entered the marketplace. But the whispers still reached her ears as she passed. In place of the glow of new love, Hannah's cheeks now burned with shame at her seeming inability to carry on her husband's name.

"When are you two going to start a family?" The innocent-sounding question seemed to cut a little deeper into my breaking heart each time it was asked. I knew this woman was simply trying to be sociable; yet rather than curiosity about when we might want to have kids, all I heard was condemnation that our marriage was not measuring up to her definition of family.

I wanted to answer that we *started* our family the day we took our wedding vows, becoming one in God's sight. I wanted to tell her of our months and years of wanting and waiting. Why must our union be validated by the addition of children before we can be counted as a family? When God created Adam and Eve, He called this family of two "very good" long before they became parents, so why couldn't I feel complete when facing these social settings?

I longed to tell her of our daughter — the one who had taken us two years to even conceive. Had Noel lived, I would have been several years a veteran of that cherished role of motherhood by now. I wanted to explain about the children who had each carried away pieces of our hearts when they did not join our family through adoption as we'd hoped.

Because I knew she was just making small talk, I chose not to allow her to glimpse the distress of my soul. I didn't want to see the stunned silence on her face. Or worse yet, to hear another round of unsolicited advice about how we should "just relax," go on vacation, or change our sexual technique. I didn't want another sarcastic offer of "Please, take my kids. They are such monsters!" along with the admonition to be thankful for my freedom.

Instead, I plastered a half-hearted smile on my face, gave a vague answer about "someday," then quickly tried to mingle with a new group of partygoers in hopes of regaining my composure before being confronted by more of the same questions another half-dozen times through the course of the evening.

In the center of the room, a throng of women swarmed the newborn in attendance with her youthful mother. Pregnant bellies seemed to fill my vision in every direction. A group of dads stood nearby, proudly boasting of their sons' recent sports victories. A coworker's snapshots of his three kids circulated through the gathering. Overwhelmed by my crushed hopes, I blinked back tears, swallowed the hard knot in my throat, and went to find my husband. My throbbing head and waves of grief-induced nausea were the perfect excuse to go home early.

Hope deferred makes the heart sick.

PROVERBS 13:12

Any discussion of infertility is incomplete unless we explore the importance of how we define *family*. A family is the most basic group in which people have always lived, and it's one of the ways in which we define ourselves and see ourselves in the context of the society around us. If we don't have a family, it is easy to feel lost or alone when surrounded by others who do. The Bible takes for granted the importance of families, with many pages spent recounting family histories and explaining who was related to whom.

Hannah's story begins with a look at her husband's family history. According to the extensive table of nations found in 1 Chronicles, Elkanah was of the priestly line. As the Levites were granted no land of their own when Israel was divided between the twelve tribes of Israel, 1 Samuel explains that Elkanah's family made its home among the Ephraimites, the descendants of Joseph. Elkanah and his family specifically lived in Ramathaim (later in the story simply called Ramah; in chapter 13 we will discover the significance of this place).

If we climb through the branches of Hannah's family tree, we learn that the Jewish nation had a tentative start. Infertility took center stage in God's account of history as the establishment and continuation of the Israelites seemed to be in question. Abraham was one hundred years old and Sarah ninety when their child of promise was finally born (see Genesis 17:17). Isaac, in turn, prayed for his barren wife, Rebekah, before God placed twins within her womb (see Genesis 25:21). One of those boys, Jacob, also went on to taste fertility challenges. While he had twelve sons, only two came from his beloved wife, Rachel, who struggled through years of infertility, both "primary" (never giving live birth) and "secondary" (unable to conceive or carry to live birth after at least one prior successful pregnancy).

I've often wondered if Rachel's first son, Joseph, might also have battled to become a father. The Bible records only two sons for him, something rare in an age without birth control, when a large family was a sign of prestige. When this beloved son of Jacob chose to name his second son Ephraim, he pronounced, "It is because God has made me fruitful in the land of my suffering" (Genesis 41:52). I find it ironic that Hannah's story, perhaps the most famous infertility story in history, is staged in the hill country of Ephraim, the land of the "twice fruitful."

The Jews took to heart God's words about children being a blessing; thus they inferred that the lack of children could only be a sign of God's disfavor. Realizing that her ancestors had also known her pain might have offered Hannah great comfort. But these same stories could have just as easily added to her burden and grief. As it became obvious to the world that God was not opening Hannah's womb as He ultimately had for her foremothers, Hannah's inability to bear a child made her a social outcast. Knowing her nation's history without seeing God answer her own pleas for a baby could well have been more discouraging than helpful.

Having children was imperative to a woman in Hannah's time. Raising sons not only provided preservation of traditions and heritage but also offered assurance and security in the event of widowhood. Without a child, there was little to no hope for a woman to be supported in her old age. Unless she was surrounded by her family, her culture gave no value to her life. Living in an industrialized nation where life insurance, Social Security, education, and job opportunities are all available to women, I cannot begin to grasp the urgency Hannah must have felt over her inability to produce heirs.

What I can relate to are many of Hannah's dreams: the desire to feel a tiny hand holding her own. The knowledge that the love expressed through her touch might bring more healing to a fevered body or a broken heart than any herb she might give. The longing to hear "Mommy, I love you" whispered in her ears, with that same voice shouting out praise songs to the Lord, delightfully off key, bringing just as much joy to her heart. The desire to be the one person who could make things "all better" for her children when the world was painful or unfair. She yearned for the taste of sweet, slobbery kisses planted on her lips in childish abandon. She longed for a family to call her own.

In those days, motherhood was an assumption and an expectation rather than something to be chosen, but dreams of bearing children likely engulfed Hannah just the same. Like any good Jewish girl, she had been raised to anticipate motherhood her entire life. When she had played with the neighborhood kids, she probably fought to have the part of "Mom" as often as she could. To raise children was her occupation of choice, with no backup plan arranged. When grown-up reality didn't measure up, her definition of *family*, her very understanding of life itself, was shaken to the core.

In her book *The Ache for a Child*, Debra Bridwell explains the devastation this way:

> God had the desire to create new life; and He wanted to create
> it in His own image. If He, being perfect and complete had this
> desire to create, how could it be selfish or wrong? And because

He created us in His image, with many of His attributes, it should come as no surprise that we share His desire to create.

If we yearn to take part in the miracle of creating a new life "in our image" with attributes like our own, and want the intimacy of nurturing our child to maturity, that is only natural. This yearning is God-given and a part of how we are created. It's no wonder that we can feel jarred and confused when we are unable to fulfill it.[1]

Seeking God's Heart Through Infertility

One of God's first instructions to the human race was to be fruitful and multiply. Scripture speaks highly of the role of parenthood. If children are a mark of God's blessing, what does infertility mean? Questions about families (growing our own, or God's view of them) seem to mount much faster than answers. As we start this journey together through Hannah's life, striving to answer some of these piercing questions, I want to be brutally honest with you about the struggles through this deep, dark valley called infertility.

While I want to be realistic, I fear painting such a bleak picture of fertility challenges that you will be left without hope. God can work great miracles, and I'm not *just* referring to the miracle of conception. If you are looking for assurance that God will give you a baby at the end of the journey, I am sorry, but I cannot offer you that promise. While He may indeed plan to add children to your life, I honestly do not believe that every couple seeking hard after God's heart is guaranteed a child. But God is a big God, big enough to heal every bitter, broken heart.

A few months after my wonderful husband first planted the idea in my mind to write this book, a close friend gave me an intriguing challenge. Julie proposed that I read through the entire Bible, looking for every passage that could in any way, directly or indirectly, relate to infertility. It seemed an overwhelming task at first, but soon I started on an exciting adventure through Scripture that would last fourteen months. There were times when the study was very painful and hard to continue — so many passages were laced with generational records. I would pray:

> Lord, one of my greatest fears is that our family tree will stop growing here. I don't want to be an old stump, cut off and cast away. The psalmist wrote, "Your wife will be like a fruitful vine within your house; your sons will be like olive shoots around your table" [Psalm 128:3]. Father, reading of your faithfulness to countless generations serves only to discourage me more. You were faithful to them — what about us? Will my husband ever have a "fruitful" wife? Will our family tree ever produce new shoots? These passages carefully explaining who begat whom, all the way back to Adam, are very painful for me.

While the shock of infertility affects each woman in a unique way, I know I was the type of woman for whom this was especially difficult. Unlike many of my friends, my career goal had always been motherhood. My earliest memories all include playing Mommy to my family of dolls, changing their diapers, serving them at tea parties, pushing them in strollers, dreaming of the day when I would have real babies to fill my arms. I adopted every stray puppy or kitten I could get my hands on, even dressing the cat in doll clothes to imagine myself one step closer to the reality of motherhood.

I've since met many, many women whose paths were different from mine. Some always thought of future motherhood as a given, yet had never focused on it until it was "time." Others had not particularly wanted children until they were surprised by this desire at age thirty, thirty-five, or even forty. But we all shared the assumption that the ability to bear children was within us, within our grasp if we chose it. We all came to a point in our lives at which our definition of *family* included children. Like Hannah, when our realities did not align with that expectation, we were all at a loss to know how to cope.

Imagine Hannah's growing grief as she began to realize that those evenings of passion shared with her sweetheart were not producing within her womb the expected results. As her childhood playmates went on to produce children of their own, Hannah continued to keep house for only two. Then the children she herself had cared for as a girl, helping out the neighborhood moms to get her "baby fixes" as often as possible, started growing up and having their own babies as well. And somewhere in the midst of this isolation and grief, her beloved Elkanah, perhaps desperate to carry on his family name, brought home a second wife. This was definitely not the definition of *family* Hannah had bargained for!

But I cry to you for help, O Lord: in the morning my prayer
comes before you. Why, O Lord, do you reject me and hide
your face from me?

Psalm 88:13-14

For Further Thought

How do you define *family*? Does your current family circumstance meet your definition? Does your definition agree with God's definition?

I can remember having terrible nightmares, waking up sobbing, dreaming that my husband had died and left me childless. These dreams demonstrated my fears and isolation of feeling that our family was far from complete. List your fears about your family as it currently is designed, then ask the Lord to help you trust Him with your worries.

Heart Treasures

The Heart Treasures sections of this book offer God's authoritative Word on aspects of each topic. Use these passages for on-your-own or group study, allowing you to dig deeper into God's heart on the matter.

Genesis 1–2

Genesis 15:1–18:15

Genesis 21:1-7

Genesis 25:19-21

Burden Bearers

> Some men came, bringing to him a paralytic, carried by four
> of them. Since they could not get him to Jesus because of the
> crowd, they made an opening in the roof above Jesus and, after
> digging through it, lowered the mat the paralyzed man was
> lying on. (Mark 2:3-4)

These friends very literally demonstrated what it means to "carry each other's burdens, and in this way you will fulfill the law of Christ" (Galatians 6:2). They met their loved one in his place of need and went out of their way to offer both practical aid for physical needs and emotional support to help him seek God through his accompanying spiritual crisis.

While the body of each chapter in this book is primarily addressed to those personally in the midst of fertility challenges, the Burden Bearers sections at the end of each chapter are created specifically for friends, families, church leaders, coworkers, and all near and dear to families facing such heartache. You are encouraged to fully read every chapter to gain understanding and then explore these special concluding portions for helpful insights.

While only some ideas may be applicable to your situation, the feelings expressed here are not uncommon to this journey and thus are written from a first-person perspective, as if told to you directly by your loved one. You may even notice a few places where your loved one has added her own notes or highlighted issues where she feels acutely vulnerable. No two people or circumstances are identical, so please use these suggestions as a springboard for thought and discussion rather than a strict guideline.

And now for the first Burden Bearer . . .

When you are meeting someone new, don't start your conversation with "So, do you have any kids?" While innocent enough, such questions can make me feel like a deer caught in your headlights. Instead try something open-ended such as "Tell me a little bit about yourself." Anyone in a less-than-ideal life circumstance (unfulfilled desires for a spouse, unemployed, and so on) will appreciate such an approach.

envy, jealousy, and rivalry

He had two wives; one was called Hannah and the other
Peninnah. Peninnah had children, but Hannah had none.

1 SAMUEL 1:2

A heart at peace gives life to the body,

but envy rots the bones.

PROVERBS 14:30

*While their union had yet to produce children, overall these had been
joyful years, full of love and blessing. Hannah longed to maintain
things as they were, to protect the exclusive bonds she had always
shared with Elkanah. But her failure to provide an heir dictated an
unpleasant change. As the day when Peninnah would join the family
drew near, Hannah's anguish escalated.*

*Though Elkanah assured her that no one else could ever take first
place in his heart, Hannah knew things could never again be quite the
same between them. She struggled with raging feelings of jealousy and
couldn't help but see this newcomer as a rival, rather than a 'sister.'
How she dreaded the inevitable day when she would see her beloved's
eyes shining with joy over the news of Peninnah's coming child. Envy
sickened her heart at the very thought.*

Hannah's dilemma illustrates one of the more sticky issues we struggle with on the path of infertility: jealousy. We are surrounded by friends, family members, and strangers who seem to have no problem conceiving and delivering healthy children. We know that envy and rivalry are not godly attributes, yet we find ourselves fighting these all the same.

As we lived through month after month without conceiving a child, I actually began to envy other women the grief of their miscarriages. I was so desperate to be a mother under any circumstances, that I begrudged the experience of losing a child. My friends could at least claim the title *mother,* even if their arms remained empty. While I am ashamed to admit such feelings, I have talked with many women who struggle with the same emotions when unable to conceive.

Rick and I experienced our first taste of fertility rivalry when my brother, Dan, and his wife, Diana, called on Valentine's Day to announce their pregnancy. We were naive enough to believe that we would be announcing our own good news always just "next month," so we weren't fully crushed at that early stage, but it was disappointing nonetheless.

Though we had begun our efforts to have a baby the previous November, we hadn't said anything to our families about our desire to conceive. But as our first anniversary came and went in August, and we planned a trip to see my new nephew, the months of negative pregnancy tests began to take their toll. It felt as if we were running a race: Dan and Diana had been given a head start while we were held back at the starting line.

Because I was not having regular menstrual cycles, I was driving to the lab every twenty-eight days for blood tests, sure that I must be pregnant *this time.* In addition to all those monthly phone calls from my doctor's office, telling me to keep trying, by the time we were just six months into the fertility race I had already taken more than a dozen home pregnancy tests, every one of them discouragingly single-lined. It was only later that I understood enough about female reproduction to realize that if I wasn't cycling, I certainly had not been consistently ovulating. So many emotional highs and lows, and there hadn't even been an opportunity for conception!

Our plan had been to surprise our loved ones with a baby announcement and only then to share some of the emotional and medical efforts that had been involved in bringing our child into the family. You may wonder if or when you should share your fertility challenges with others. Decisions about if, when, or with whom to share your heartache should be made with care. Each time you share your story, you are taking a risk, not knowing if your listener will be supportive, understanding, dismissive, or critical. Rick and I came from strong Christian backgrounds and had every reason to anticipate supportive responses from our loved ones.

By the time Diana's due date grew close, we were just beginning infertility treatment and decided it was time to tell our families about our struggles. Their reactions were mixed. Susan, my closest friend, who filled the role of a sister, exclaimed, "Happy parenthood!" choosing to hope with us that our doctor's prediction of pregnancy within my first six months on the fertility drug Clomid would be correct. My mom, counting the days until the birth of her first grandson, was supportive, yet didn't fully grasp our frustrations.

When my brother learned our news in that first sleep-deprived week as a new father, his greatest concern was for my health, wondering if his little sister really knew what she was doing by taking fertility medications. Rick's brother and sister-in-law urged us to treasure our time as a family of two and not to rush into parenthood. Rick's dad, caught off guard that a couple so young and financially unestablished would even consider parenthood, actually announced that he was praying we would not have children any time soon.

For a long time I was angry at the very thought of Rick's dad praying against our desires. While I knew that his reaction was one of genuine surprise and concern, I blamed Dad's prayer whenever we seemed to fall another step behind in the baby quest. Like the sincere followers of Christ who have pleaded for victory on opposing sides of countless bloody battlefields through the course of history, I thought our petitions so negated one another that it would be impossible for us each to receive our desired requests. God knew that each of our prayers was born of passionate convictions, yet I ached to know to whom He would listen.

I still don't fully understand how the conflicting prayers of believers play out in the heavenly realm. Part of the picture may be answered in Romans 8:26-27: "In the same way, the Spirit helps us in our weakness. We do not know what we ought to pray for, but the Spirit himself intercedes for us with groans that words cannot express. And he who searches our hearts knows the mind of the Spirit, because the Spirit intercedes for the saints in accordance with God's will."

God knows our hearts, desires, and longings. He also longs for us to experience His best for our lives. When we pray, our requests, fraught as they are with our clouded perspectives and sinful human natures, are in essence "filtered" through the Holy Spirit. While it might seem frustrating that our prayers are no longer entirely our own, having God Himself interceding on our behalf is an incredible privilege.

As I tried to persuade God to give us a child on my terms, we watched my nephew grow from baby, to toddler, and into little boy. We continued to be held back at the starting gate as Rick's brother and sister-in-law welcomed a son. Then a third nephew came along. *Wait! When did the starting gun fire? How did everyone else get so far ahead in this race?*

Our brothers weren't the only ones winning prizes in the fertility marathon. It seemed that every woman I saw was either nine months pregnant or pushing a baby stroller. I began dreading my trips to the grocery store, where I would invariably see women with gobs of kids stuffed into shopping carts, hanging from their arms, and running about their feet.

Many of these moms didn't seem happy with their blessings either. When I would hear a mother yelling obscenities at her child just for acting like a normal kid, it was all I could do to keep myself from committing child theft. I kept wondering what criteria God was using in the allotment of offspring.

My anger and jealousy flared as I observed so many heartbreaking situations. Some of the emotions were righteous anger, like that demonstrated when Jesus drove the tax collectors from His temple. Many more were rooted in prideful envy.

Why would God allow the girl across the street to have three abortions by her sixteenth birthday, while we remained barren? Where would the seventeen-year-old, single teenager in our church, without so much as a high school diploma, find the resources to care for the baby we longed to adopt? How could a just God knowingly send children into abusive situations rather than fill our empty arms?

In short, I felt I knew better than God. I called Him to account for decisions that made no sense from my limited perspective. Here we were, a happily married Christian couple following all the rules. We had been obedient to the Lord, waiting to offer the gift of our virginity to one another on our wedding night. We were serving the Lord through full-time ministry and active involvement in our church.

While we didn't have much money, we had a stable income and had created an inviting home from the empty shell of our tiny apartment. We longed to give our children a lifetime of love, training them in the nurture and admonition of the Lord. Believing that I would make a better mother than so many who were given the chance, I felt that we had earned the right of parenthood. Didn't God owe us something here?

Surprisingly, the answer was, and is, no. God does not owe me anything: not a baby, not even an explanation of His choices. As Hannah endured years of social inferiority as a barren wife, she had no way to know that God's ultimate plan was to bless her with a special son whom He would use to lead His people. To look at my current circumstances and accuse God of making a mistake would be like trying to see a finished picture in a single piece of a complex puzzle. The blurs of color are senseless on their own, but when my piece is placed with all the rest, the entire beautiful masterpiece is pulled together. God sees the big picture from beginning to end. I can only see my little piece right now.

When God's Plans Don't Seem to Make Sense

If God doesn't condone sexual relations outside marriage, why does He often create new life from these unions? When a godly family is eagerly waiting for a baby, why does He sometimes withhold? In our it's-all-about-me society, it can be easy to lose sight of the fact that God's choice to place a baby in a womb may have as much to do with His plans for that child as for the mother herself.

God perfectly orchestrates the necessary timing for each new life to fulfill the plans He ordains. Had God given Hannah a child when she first desired motherhood, would she have ever dedicated Samuel to His service? This child was called to an office of great leadership for the good of an entire nation, but in order to prepare both Hannah's heart and the circumstances that would lead Samuel to anoint kings, heartache had to come first.

A friend once described her emotions when her unmarried, drug-addicted sister announced her third unwise pregnancy. In the midst of her grief, I was encouraged to hear victory through Christ. She focused on the way our amazing God can use the same circumstances differently in two lives, depending on the lessons He is striving to teach each. While childlessness is a trial for infertile couples and we consider parenthood a great blessing, for others pregnancy might indeed be the trial that God uses to change their hearts.

Two Bible stories come to mind here. An angel said to unloved Hagar, "You are now with child . . . for the LORD has heard of your misery" (Genesis 16:11). And of Jacob's wife, the Scriptures say, "When the LORD saw that Leah was not loved, he opened her womb" (29:31). While it can be anguish for us to watch, I think sometimes God allows those "unloved" women in our lives the gift/trial of pregnancy to demonstrate His love to them.

Think of someone you know who is pregnant when she didn't want to be — a single mom, a woman in a rocky marriage, a hardened career woman who never intended to become a mother, a friend or sister who conceives at the drop of a hat. Just as God may want to use my empty arms to bring me closer to Himself, God may challenge another woman I don't feel "deserves" a baby with such a gift so that He can ultimately remind her that He is still God.

"For my thoughts are not your thoughts, neither are your ways my ways," declares the LORD. "As the heavens are higher than the earth, so are my ways higher than your ways and my thoughts than your thoughts."

ISAIAH 55:8-9

The members of our church seemed caught in a perpetual baby boom. Most were young newlyweds like ourselves. Some had three or four kids in as many years. Time after time, I was invited to another baby shower. Each was a setup for envious heartache. In addition to my own misery, the guest of honor and other shower attendees walked on eggshells around me.

After making a blubbering fool of myself at one especially disastrous shower, I stopped attending them altogether. While I longed to rejoice with those who were rejoicing, my envy was too strong. It was not worth the emotional toll or the spiritual setbacks to continue attending events that only made me focus on what I did not have.

I vividly remember the day a friend showed up at church in tears, having just learned that she was pregnant with her third child. Neither of her first two babies (who were still in diapers) had been planned, and this newest addition was a surprise as well. Her fears about providing for another hungry mouth when they already struggled to make ends meet were valid, but I saw her reaction as ungratefulness for the very gift I so yearned to receive. I was jealous that God would give her what she did not even want, and hurt that she should show anything but joy over such a treasure. *Lord, did you mix up the order? Wasn't this baby supposed to be for me?*

In my first few years of marriage, I only knew two other women dealing with fertility challenges. One friend had miscarried her first baby a couple of years before we met and had been unable to conceive since. Another woman from our church had been blessed with two living children, nearly ten years apart, and had suffered multiple miscarriages before and after each. Both women longed for more children but seemed willing to submit to the Lord's perfect will if that was not His plan for their lives.

I could not understand the peace my friends portrayed in the midst of broken dreams. Having gone through so much more loss than I had yet experienced, how could either of them seem to handle the pain so well when I was grieving so deeply? Rather than drawing from their strength, I found my faith floundering. When each moment, hour, day, and week seemed to break my heart a little more, I truly felt I would die if God asked me to endure years of childlessness.

In hindsight, I now see that the peace that frightened me in these women was not an indifference to heartaches. Rather they displayed maturity refined by God's work in their hearts through the fire of their pain. They had learned the secret of drawing their strength from the Lord instead of fighting Him with every breath they drew.

While I do not know how long your journey will last, I promise that if you are seeking God in the midst of the pain, you will not always hurt with the intensity you may be feeling right now. While the time frame is different for each person, the most painful years of my infertility journey were the first two, especially from about six to eighteen months. On the other hand, my friend Julie Donohue (who founded the online infertility ministry Ladies In Waiting) didn't begin to wonder why she wasn't getting pregnant until several years without birth control or conception had passed. Julie points out that for each of us infertility was a "mindset." Our *realizations* that we might have problems having children came about much differently.

I began to *feel* infertile almost from our first cycle without conception, each month growing more anxious than the one before. Julie was medically infertile long before the questions and emotions followed. We took on the roles of infertile women at different extremes in the continuum, but once we each began to grieve, God carried both of us through very similar steps from heartache to hope. This healing was well underway long before He granted either of us the gift of a child.

Do not be anxious about anything, but in everything, by prayer
and petition, with thanksgiving, present your requests to God.
And the peace of God, which transcends all understanding,
will guard your hearts and your minds in Christ Jesus.

PHILIPPIANS 4:6-7

For Further Thought

While commonly thought of as synonymous, *envy* and *jealousy* carry subtle, yet significant, distinctions. While God created us with a vast range of emotions, some expressions of these emotions do not bring Him glory. It is important not to let feelings rage out of control, ruling all of life.

Envy represents resentment of what others have, selfishness, covetousness, greed, and desire for gain at the cost of another. It distorts the truth to validate or intensify its own perspective of pain. A sobering reminder of envy's power is found in Matthew's account of the crucifixion: "For [Pilate] knew it was out of envy that they had handed Jesus over to him" (27:18). If envy drove those who murdered our Lord, it is an emotion I want to carefully commit to God whenever I find it in my own heart.

Like envy, *jealousy* can involve anger and a defensive spirit, but unlike envy, it can be expressed in both positive and negative ways. Jealousy involves a protective element, a desire to grasp tightly that which seems rightfully mine. Ungodly jealousy indignantly demands its own way, such as my "right" to motherhood. An example of righteous jealousy would be the passionate protection of my marriage against outside threat.

Heart Treasures

Exodus 34:14

Proverbs 27:4

2 Corinthians 11:1-4

James 4:5

1 Peter 2:1

Burden Bearers

Realize that investing in a relationship with me may be costly. I do not mean to be hard to live with right now, but because I am hurting, I may unintentionally hurt you in self-defense. "If only my anguish could be weighed and all my misery be placed on the scales! It would surely outweigh the sand of the seas — no wonder my words have been impetuous" (Job 6:2-3).

If you are in the process of attempting to conceive, ask how I would like to receive your news. (I may prefer face-to-face contact, a brief phone call, a note in the mail, or to have a mutual friend tell me on your behalf so that I can work out my grief privately before contacting you to share your joy.) If you are already expecting and don't know how to tell me, please find some way to quietly inform me before your joy becomes public knowledge, so that your news isn't sprung on me in public, where I may be unable to cope.

is God punishing me?

Year after year this man went up from his town to worship and sacrifice to the LORD Almighty at Shiloh, where Hophni and Phinehas, the two sons of Eli, were priests of the LORD. Whenever the day came for Elkanah to sacrifice, he would give portions of the meat to his wife Peninnah and to all her sons and daughters.

1 SAMUEL 1:3-4

Before this faith came, we were held prisoners by the law, locked up until faith should be revealed. So the law was put in charge to lead us to Christ that we might be justified by faith. Now that faith has come, we are no longer under the supervision of the law.

GALATIANS 3:23-25

Hannah's feet dragged under the weight of her heavy heart. How many years had she faithfully made this trip with the man she loved? The undulating route north wasn't terribly lengthy, maybe fifteen miles or so. But their venture took so much longer now, with Elkanah's growing family to slow their progress. As the hilly path stretched before them, once again Hannah wondered how much more pleasure she would take in this walk; if only she could bear the load of her own sleepy child hoisted on one hip.

How could she survive another day of worship and feasting when joy eluded her? Like birthdays, anniversaries, and other holiday landmarks, this yearly expedition to Shiloh echoed the loud and relentless reminders of her biological clock's ticking. For yet another year she faced the disheartening reality that she might never be a mother.

While her husband remained true to the Lord, many of their countrymen had turned their backs on God, neglecting His commandments and journeys such as this. The law did not require women to make this pilgrimage, yet Hannah faithfully walked by her husband's side, longing to find favor with her God. Surely the Lord seemed pleased with Elkanah, as evidenced by Peninnah's abundant fertility. What had Hannah done to anger God enough that He would curse her so?

God had promised His people that "none would miscarry or be barren" in Israel (Exodus 23:26). So what was a woman like Hannah to think as the years passed her by without the sound of her baby's first cry? Is infertility a punishment for sin?

Read through Old Testament Law, such as the book of Numbers, searching for words like *barren* and *miscarry,* and you will find a depressing list of sins that would directly result in empty wombs. Considering the heavy regulations of the Law, Hannah's contemporaries had reasonable grounds to look at her empty arms and conclude (albeit wrongly) that God was punishing her.

Under the Law, could God use infertility as punishment for sin? Absolutely! Was this the case for Hannah? Scripture seems clear that it was not. While Hannah may have burdened herself with guilt, her barrenness was not recorded to be condemnation for her personal sins.

The Law required the Israelites to worship God and do all He had commanded in order for God's protection and blessings to be poured out on them. The promises to Israel were to the nation as a whole, for corporate obedience. Many of Hannah's people had strayed far from God, seeking after idols and abandoning the God who had promised so much, including fruitful wombs. Their very leadership was corrupted as Hophni and Phinehas made mockery of the priesthood (see 1 Samuel 2:12-17), negating God's promised blessings for all.

Hannah was not alone in enduring both heartache and misunderstanding about the role of sin in her suffering. Consider Job: "This man was blameless and upright; he feared God and shunned evil" (Job 1:1). So God rewarded Job's faithfulness by giving him a life free from suffering, right? Anything but! God allowed Satan to take everything from Job, including the lives of his children, his great wealth, his health, and even the understanding of friends. "In all this, Job did not sin" (2:10).

We see another example of grief without blame in the gospel of Luke:

> In the time of Herod king of Judea there was a priest named Zechariah, who belonged to the priestly division of Abijah; his wife Elizabeth was also a descendant of Aaron. *Both of them were upright in the sight of God, observing all the Lord's commandments and regulations blamelessly.* But they had no children, because Elizabeth was barren; and they were both well along in years. (Luke 1:5-7, emphasis added)

"Well, that's nice for them," you may think, "but I still know God must be judging me for my sins." I regularly hear stories from women anguished over their past: abuse, sexual relations outside marriage, abortion, substance usage. It absolutely breaks my heart to read statements like this: "I have just learned from my doctor I am sterile. I know God is punishing me for the abortion I had as a teenager. How can I cope with the guilt of killing the only child my body could ever bear?"

Do you have a similar story? If so, I urge you to take God at His Word. Scripture tells us, "If we confess our sins, he is faithful and just and will forgive us our sins and purify us from all unrighteousness" (1 John 1:9). My dad puts it this way: "When I confess my sins, God is faithful to forgive me and to give me a spiritual bath."

Paul, once a murderer and more, wrote, "Here is a trustworthy saying that deserves full acceptance: Christ Jesus came into the world to save sinners — of whom I am the worst. But for that very reason I was shown mercy so that in me, the worst of sinners, Christ Jesus might display his unlimited patience as an example for those who would believe on him and receive eternal life" (1 Timothy 1:15-16).

No sin is too big. If you have admitted your past to God and repented, He has already offered His forgiveness, and He desires to wash you clean of guilt. Will you accept? And if the God of all the universe has forgiven you, is your standard of righteousness higher than His? By refusing to forgive yourself, is this not insulting our sovereign God?

I imagine that you have some kind of relationship with God that would prompt you to want to learn more about a biblical figure like Hannah. But not knowing exactly what your background may be, I want to be clear about what is required to receive God's grace. If you move on from this chapter without squarely facing the state of your relationship with God, the impact of the rest of this book will be greatly hampered.

God's grace is *not* about getting some spiritual formula right, or being good enough to deserve His forgiveness, or even saying the proper words of some mystical prayer. I am not sharing any religion here; rather, I'm extending God's invitation to join Him in a personal relationship where He will listen to the cries of your heart. Believing there *is* a God is a good start, but belief alone is not enough (see James 2:19). Forgiveness must be *accepted* to be of any benefit.

The Law that bound Hannah was established for the purpose of showing us that God's measure of perfect holiness is a standard too high for any human to obtain. The Bible states it simply: "All have sinned and fall short of the glory of God" (Romans 3:23). We *all* have sins that justly deserve God's wrath. No one is good enough for God. And just as we cannot be good enough to deserve God's grace, we cannot be bad enough to be unforgivable. No matter what your past, God's grace is bigger than your guilt.

Your fertility challenges hurt this much because you already have a mother's heart and are grieving for your children. God knows this grief personally. He has gone to greater measures to make you His child than you will ever go in the pursuit of growing your own family. John 3:16 is a classic Bible verse that many of us have heard since childhood. But have you ever stopped to really think about what this verse is saying? I like to paraphrase it this way: "For God so longed to call me His child, that He offered the life of His only biological Son to pay the price of my adoption."

God's Son, Jesus Christ, was the only man to ever live without sin. By willingly taking the ultimate punishment for my sins through His torturous assignation on the cross, He has already paid the penalty for all my regrets. Through His shed blood on the cross and His victory over the grave, Jesus Christ moved us into the era of grace. When we carry our guilt and believe we caused God to send infertility into our lives, we are buying into the lies of the Accuser. Satan came to kill, steal, and destroy (see John 10:10). Christ came to set us free from the Law.

Hannah's peers may have been able to look at Scripture and draw cause-and-effect-conclusions that God was using her womb to punish her for some deep, dark sin. But "Christ is the end of the law" (Romans 10:4). We are no longer prisoners to the Law, praise be to God!

If you are feeling imprisoned by your past, please take time now to truly deal with these issues before God. If you are questioning the very reality of God, ask Him to make Himself known to you. He promised, "You will seek me and find me when you seek me with all your heart" (Jeremiah 29:13). Confess to Him those mistakes that are causing you grief. Ask for His forgiveness. Give Him the weight of your guilt. Thank Him for paying the penalty for your sins by giving the life of His Son.

───────────

He does not treat us as our sins deserve or repay us according
to our iniquities.

PSALM 103:10

───────────

When He Doesn't Intervene

Just as God lifted His hedge of protection from the entire nation of Israel when some turned their backs on Him, He sometimes chooses not to intervene in the natural course of events in our lives too. Poor choices may carry lifetime consequences, but these consequences need to be seen for exactly what they are: natural results, not punishments. We have a tendency to expect the easy road when, in fact, the times God chooses to prevent tragedies are seasons of undeserved grace.

Trials and heartaches are nondiscriminatory. God "causes his sun to rise on the evil and the good, and sends rain on the righteous and the unrighteous" (Matthew 5:45). To say that all people who lose lives, loved ones, or possessions in disasters such as fires, floods, and earthquakes are being judged by God is ridiculous, yet when fertility challenges hit home, the first answer we seek is where to place the blame. Even if assigning blame can't fix our problem, somehow it just makes us feel better to come up with a reason *why*.

God has the power to prevent your grief, but when He chooses not to, this is not an automatic sign that you are being punished. With so many families dealing with infertility and loss, you may be simply swept up in an epidemic. Several entire books are written on the single topic of why God allows bad things to happen to good people. Your empty womb may be a "bad thing" that doesn't have a specific source of blame.

If you have confessed your sins to God and accepted His freely offered forgiveness, He has become your Father and you are His child. As your perfect, loving, just Daddy, He does not desire to cause you to suffer. As much as I grieve with each hurting heart, I know God hurts with you even more.

A Time of Testing

For men are not cast off by the Lord forever. Though he brings grief, he will show compassion, so great is his unfailing love. For he does not willingly bring affliction or grief to the children of men. (Lamentations 3:31-33)

The above passage sounds so pretty, talking of God's compassion and love and not wanting to bring heartache. But wait. What does it say about God "bringing grief"? Doesn't that contradict the concept of God *allowing* the natural progression of consequences, not punishing me?

While I cannot find a theological basis to say that God is punishing you through infertility, I cannot discount the possibility that, as He did in my own life, He may desire to use your time of testing to reveal heart issues that still need to be addressed before Him. God often uses trials to get our attention when we need to draw closer to Him.

As Hannah probably did, we need to evaluate our lives for unconfessed sins that may be standing between us and the Lord. At the very least, sin breaks our fellowship with God, making trials significantly harder to endure because we face them in our own strength.

While Satan imprisons some with bondage to past sins, he can entangle others in what seems to be a good and righteous goal, causing them to lose sight of God in the midst of self-evaluation. Do not become so caught up in an ongoing quest to uncover "hidden sin" that this pursuit becomes an end in itself. I fell into the trap of believing that if I could only find that one thing that was keeping me from right fellowship with God and "fix it," then of course God would fill my arms right away.

Conviction of sin is the work of the Holy Spirit. When I ask Him to reveal those issues He wants to address in my life, I know that He will show me what I need to know about my own heart. I do not need to dwell on finding something God is not yet ready to address with me. Confession should come from a heart desire to renew right fellowship with God, not as a bargaining tool to seek a release from trials.

We are called to be *disciples* of Jesus, followers under the discipline of God. *Discipline* is vastly different from *punishment*. A criminal receives punishment by the courts. A solider or an athlete understands the need for discipline in order to accomplish goals. Whereas *punishment* represents penalty or retribution, discipline's goal is to train, mold, and perfect. While I do not believe God is punishing you, it is possible that He desires to use this time of heartache as a season of discipline in your life, if only you will let Him.

Discipline is often painful (just think how your muscles feel the morning after you start a new exercise routine), but it is an ongoing part of the Christian walk. A young child who can read at elementary school levels should be proud of his accomplishment, but if a college student is still reading only with the comprehension of a second-grader, there is a problem. Our relationship with God is the same way.

As a child of God, I am living a continual process of spiritual growth and maturity. In God's grace, He does things in stages, not expecting a kinder-gartener to pass college exams. For the rest of my life God will be striving to remake my old self into someone patterned after Himself. Fertility challenges can yield great growth if I seek hard after God through my pain.

Endure hardship as discipline; God is treating you as sons. For what son is not disciplined by his father? If you are not disciplined (and everyone undergoes discipline), then you are illegitimate children and not true sons.

HEBREWS 12:7-8

For Further Thought

The issue of abortion can be devastatingly painful to any woman dealing with fertility challenges, either from personal experience or from grief that God could allow any baby's life to be taken when she so longs for a child. (*Rain Dance* by Joy DeKok is a tremendously realistic, fictional look at both sides of this heartache. Due to the topic, I resisted reading this book for a long time, but am so glad I finally did, and I highly recommend it.)

I often feared God wasn't allowing me to become a mother because He knew ahead of time that I wouldn't do a good job. I felt God was withholding from me for things that hadn't even happened. I now think of this unrealistic view of God's working as "pre-guilt." In what areas do you struggle with pre-guilt?

Heart Treasures

Leviticus 23

1 Samuel 2:12-17

Job 1-2

Psalm 139:23-24

Proverbs 15:32

Romans 5:3-8

Romans 6

Galatians 3

Philippians 3:9

Hebrews 12:10-11

Revelation 3:19

Burden Bearers

Please don't tell me I am being punished. I am already probing my heart with a microscope to see if there are any offensive ways standing in the way of my relationship with God.

Infertility and bereavement carry many painful emotions, often including a false sense of guilt and self-blame. Please be careful not to try to play the role of the Holy Spirit in my life. If you truly believe my fertility challenges are entangled with sin issues, prayerfully approach me with loving-kindness rather than condemnation, in keeping with Matthew 18, Galatians 6, and James 5:19-20.

because he loved her

But to Hannah [Elkanah] gave a double portion because he loved her, and the LORD had closed her womb.

1 SAMUEL 1:5

In this same way, husbands ought to love their wives as their own bodies. He who loves his wife loves himself.

EPHESIANS 5:28

While Elkanah and Hannah could only speculate as to why God had allowed the disabling of Hannah's reproductive abilities, His decision flooded their hearts with a wide range of emotions, all deeper than they had ever dreamed possible. At times this shared sorrow brought out the worst in each of them. Other moments were blessed in ways they might never have known, were it not for this crisis. While they sometimes stepped on one another's toes, Elkanah and Hannah found that their anguish frequently served to strengthen their marriage bonds.

While Hannah grieved for a baby, Elkanah battled his own heartaches. Peninnah had finally helped him overcome the need to prove himself virile, yet fatherhood could be a painful reminder that he had compromised the strength of the union with his beloved Hannah. The frustration of seeing his wife wounded while being unable to remove her source of distress was crushing.

I once heard that infertility is like a roller coaster where the wife is struggling to hold on during the wild ride while her husband is frantically trying to find the brake. Infertility is not just a "woman's issue." It affects both wives and husbands, though often in surprisingly different ways. Wives sometimes have a hard time understanding the unique difficulties their husbands face when dealing with infertility. In this chapter I'll try to illuminate some of the challenges guys face, in the hopes of helping you keep your marriage strong through complicated times.

Understanding Your Husband's Perspective

Little frustrates a man more than feeling inadequate to prevent his wife's pain. First of all, most guys want to "fix it." It's part of their nature and how God made them. When they can't, they often feel they at least need to "be strong."

Wives, sometimes you may not appreciate your husband's strength. It may seem that he doesn't care as much as you do or that he's not sensitive or grieving with you. He may even seem stoic. This is probably not the case. Oftentimes men deal with their grief, sadness, or helplessness in the only way they know how: through being strong. If we understand this, we will have more appreciation for how God created our husbands, and we will avoid the additional heartache of unrealistic expectations.

Husbands, it may surprise you to know that, while your wife depends on your strength, your vulnerability can be a great treasure to her as well. Knowing the depth of your sorrow, anger, or frustration will comfort her, because it means she is not dealing with those emotions alone. I encourage you to share your feelings with her and trust that she can handle it even in the midst of her own emotional journey.

Christie and her husband, Glen, had just suffered their second stillbirth when she wrote,

> Today was bittersweet. My husband and I spent the whole day just the two of us. We wrote letters to Simon and buried them

with his ashes under a tree by a waterfall. For the first time our roles were reversed as I was feeling strong and he broke down. There is a peculiar intimacy in grieving together, but I feel badly that I am comforted by his grief. It's hard to see him hurting this way. There were so many things he wanted to do with his boys — teaching them to play hockey, to shave, how to treat girls.

While infertility, miscarriage, stillbirth, and adoption loss can be some of the most painful experiences we endure, our marriages can be made stronger when we have the courage to share these most vulnerable moments with one another.

For Men Only: Collection Time

When marriages are suffering infertility, both partners usually need to be tested. For men, this brings up the necessity of . . . *The Sample*. Who can blame a guy for not being excited about collecting in a lonely, cold bathroom? Or worse yet, to be encouraged to obtain the needed specimen with the aid of pornography — a definite problem for any Christian.

The first time we were confronted with the need to obtain a semen sample for testing, Rick refused to collect. I was hurt. *If I have to go through all these tests, humiliating procedures, surgeries, medications, and pain, the least he could do is give a little sample!* The root of the issue was my husband's strong convictions against masturbation. God laid something on his heart, and he stood firm to that conviction even when he knew I was unhappy. I fussed and pouted and whined, but nothing changed. I'm sure Rick must have considered giving into my demands just to get me off his case, but he remained faithful to what he believed. While I was angry at the time, my admiration for him grew by leaps and bounds as I saw his steadfastness.

God finally got my attention and reminded me that He had assigned Rick to be the spiritual head of our household. While the Lord had not placed the same conviction against masturbation in all cases on my heart, this did not invalidate His leading in Rick's life. I had the power to build Rick up or to become a stumbling block. Rick's decisions weren't mine to control, but my reactions were.

Once I finally confessed my rebellious attitudes, God quickly brought an amazing answer to prayer. We discovered a product called a fertility condom, also known as a "condom for insemination" or "Seminal Collection Device" (SCD). This tool allows a couple to collect together, through intercourse, in the natural setting of their own home (or a hotel room near the doctor's office). Now we could obtain our sample without compromising Rick's convictions. (See appendix B on page 213 for more information about SCDs.)

Cast all your anxiety on him because he cares for you.

1 PETER 5:7

Unfaithfulness: The Side Effect Nobody Talks About

Before we go on, I beg your indulgence in a side note of sisterly concern. Failure to conceive, recurrent loss, the death of a child — all these hit at the core of a marriage relationship. Both spouses may struggle to feel "manly" or "womanly" enough. The marriage can feel like a sad or lonely place. It is easy to strive to fill these voids outside the marriage union.

Many couples willing to discuss the realities of infertility-related marital stress admit to some level of infidelity on the part of one or both partners. As shocking as this may sound, remember God sees faithfulness as a heart issue, not just a physical act: "But I tell you that anyone who looks at a woman lustfully has already committed adultery with her in his heart" (Matthew 5:28). Be it tangible or fantasy, the sin is just as real.

For some, this unfaithfulness may be as seemingly innocent as feeding your mind on unrealistic romance novels. A vast percentage, including a growing number of women, admit at least one slip into pornography, if not ongoing abuse. Many are hit by the very real temptation to seek fulfillment outside the bonds of marriage, sharing intimacies of the heart and sometimes of the body with a member of the opposite sex.

I write this troubling news with a three-fold intent. First, if you have discovered your spouse to be living a lie, your story is not unique. I am not condoning these activities, but it is important to know you are far from alone. Your husband or wife is accountable to God for this sin. You do not bear the guilt. Find someone in whom to confide (preferably of your own sex, so you aren't setting yourself up for the same sin), and seek prayer support and counsel.

If you are seeing in yourself any warning signs that you have overstepped the bonds of your marriage vows, be it in a physical act or in thought or conversation, my second reason to share is for you. It is time to be free of this burden! Confess your sin to the Lord. Pray for forgiveness, then for wisdom and strength to be honest with your spouse.

My suggestion that your marriage could fall victim to such sins may horrify you. Or you may have stumbled in the past, been forgiven, and now feel this trap to be safely behind you. My third point involves Proverbs 4:23: "Above all else, guard your heart, for it is the wellspring of life." Neither of you is immune to temptation. Marriage is built on trust, so I'm not suggesting you need to police your partner. I'm encouraging ongoing communication. *Talk* to one another frequently, even about the hard issues such as these. And *pray* for and with each other that your marriage may be a safe haven for you both.

So, if you think you are standing firm, be careful that you don't fall! No temptation has seized you except what is common to man. And God is faithful; he will not let you be tempted beyond what you can bear. But when you are tempted, he will also provide a way out so that you can stand up under it.

1 CORINTHIANS 10:12-13

Does My Spouse Love Me Only for My Fertility?

Remember Leah, who felt she needed to earn her husband's love (see Genesis 29–30)? With each pregnancy she announced sentiments like "Surely my husband will love me now. . . . At last my husband will become attached to me, because I have borne him three sons. . . . This time my husband will treat me with honor, because I have borne him six sons."

Scripture is clear that God's ideal for marriage is one man and one woman for a lifetime. Yes, divorce grieves His heart, yet early religious leaders twisted Scripture to say that man was *required* to "be fruitful and multiply," even to the point of divorcing a barren wife after ten years.[1] While I'm repulsed at the very thought of polygamy, Elkanah's taking of Peninnah as an additional wife, not as a replacement, was actually an act of great mercy. He affirmed his love for Hannah, with or without children.

When Elkanah offered Hannah a double portion of the sacrificial feast, perhaps he was alluding to traditional distributions of inheritance. In biblical times, a double portion of an estate was given to the oldest male heir. No woman had a part in the legacy, but among all male children, the firstborn was to receive twice the blessings, status, and material goods given to his brothers. For a woman to be given enough for her own offering, as well as an extra portion for the child she did not have, would have been an uncommon grace. What a contrast between Jacob's attitude toward Leah and the loving grace Elkanah showered on Hannah.

Husbands, love your wives, just as Christ loved the church and gave himself up for her.
EPHESIANS 5:25

We went into marriage knowing that it might be hard to grow our family. I had a long history of female issues, and Rick takes medication that can sometimes result in sterility. We were pleasantly surprised by wonderful test results for Rick as my list of known problems continued to mount. While grateful that we were not facing dual diagnoses, I struggled with the knowledge that if Rick had only married the "right" woman, he could have already been a father. Families with male factor infertility often deal with these same feelings in reverse.

One of the most loving gifts Rick ever gave me was his ongoing assurance that infertility was our battle, not my humiliation to bear alone. God knew from the start that it would take ten years and giving our hearts to a dozen children before we would bring two safely home. While it was my body that complicated our efforts, Rick frequently reminded me that as one flesh before God, there was no his or hers. God's plans for us as a couple included wrestling to build our family.

The man said, "This is now bone of my bones and flesh of my flesh; she shall be called 'woman,' for she was taken out of man."

GENESIS 2:23

For Further Thought

Ask the Lord to show you tangible ways to minister to your husband or wife in the midst of this journey. As you place his or her needs above your own, your marriage will deepen.

For wives: List some specific ways your husband has treated you with grace in the midst of grief. How has he been strong for you? In what ways has he shared his sorrow?

For husbands: List some ways you might minister to your wife. Here are some ways that I felt honored and blessed by Rick:

Rick trusts me with glimpses of his own vulnerability. While rare and sobering to see my husband in tears, his willingness to occasionally come out of "protector mode" validates my own sorrow, anger, and grief.

Rick takes note of dates significant to me (would-have-been due dates, anniversaries of our losses, and so on) and makes a point to recognize my pain on these days.

He prays for and with me. In addition to the ongoing regular prayer support, two specific events stand out in my mind. Once he came home very late from Bible study, woke me up, placed his hands over my womb, and passionately poured out our broken hearts to the Lord. Another time he committed himself to forty days of prayer and fasting on behalf of our longing for children.

He listened to my years of hormonally driven rants and tears, often setting aside his God-given fix-it drive to just listen, hold me, and let me cry.

He sought resources for me and supported me in creating resources for others.

He invested in my heart and learned what makes me tick. When we miscarried two babies within four months, Rick came home early from work with a rosebush to plant in our yard. Rather than asking me to endure that weekend's Mother's Day church service, he whisked me off to a quiet getaway. This past Christmas he gave me a necklace bearing the birthstones of all five of our biological children, those on earth and those in heaven.

Heart Treasures

Psalm 33:11

Proverbs 16:1

Jeremiah 29:11

1 Corinthians 6:18-20

1 Corinthians 8

Burden Bearers (For Guys)

Realize that even when I may not express myself verbally, I am still hurting. The most common question a father who has lost a child typically hears is "How is your wife?" Remember, I'm grieving too.

Please don't tease me about our struggles. While I might laugh with the guys when you talk about how I'm "shooting blanks," inside I'm cringing. Infertility procedures, such as providing sperm samples or having surgery on very private parts of my anatomy, can be highly embarrassing and cause great spiritual or emotional conflicts.

Don't make presumptions or pretend to know what I'm dealing with, unless you know the specifics of my circumstances and have lived through this yourself. Infertility is statistically caused just as often by male factors as by female factors, but even in male factor cases I may feel virtually pushed out of the loop once serious treatments begin. Sometimes I feel like my wife sees more of her doctor than of her own husband.

put yourself in my shoes (before you put your foot in your mouth)

And because the LORD had closed her womb, her rival kept provoking her in order to irritate her.

1 SAMUEL 1:6

I have become a laughingstock to my friends, though I called upon God and he answered—a mere laughingstock, though righteous and blameless!

JOB 12:4

Hannah found herself uncommonly sensitive to the words and actions of family, friends, acquaintances, even strangers. She longed for a friend with whom she could freely share both laughter and tears without ever having to explain or defend herself. While she strove to leave her longings with God, those around her often complicated this task.

She couldn't decide what hurt more. Acquaintances who seemed truly oblivious to the very existence of her pain? Loved ones who knew her anguish well, yet ignored the situation, as if not mentioning grief would make it disappear? Or well-intentioned friends who brought heartache with ill-timed words and misplaced platitudes?

While Hannah could overlook many of the missteps taken by those who attempted to walk beside her through this season, Peninnah's intentional cruelty was another story. That woman seemed to go out of her way to crush Hannah's spirit.

"I am so tired of people asking how far along I was when I lost Andrew and then acting as if he was not even a baby," writes Tracey. "I don't understand why people act so different when I tell them I was eighteen weeks. I delivered a stillborn child that I wanted very, very badly. . . . He was perfectly formed and just beautiful. We held him and have pictures and hand and feet prints. We had a funeral, and he is buried in the cemetery next to our family members. I am so shocked at the words and actions of people. This is so real to us. We love Andrew just like our two living sons."

As difficult as it is to cope with struggles in childbearing, our well-meaning friends and family members can make it even more challenging. People who haven't walked in our shoes have no idea of the depths to which we grieve and experience anger and hopelessness. It's no wonder their comments and behaviors can often seem insensitive or downright clueless.

Making it worse, the loved ones of infertile couples often feel they must measure every word and action, yet will be attacked the moment they make an unintentional slip up. A friend who watched her brother go through infertility shared her frustration over the "politically correct" mindset of infertile families, who seem to take every word or act of those with living children as a personal threat or challenge.

While, sadly, there are a few vindictive individuals who may set out to use my grief against me, most of the scenarios that bring me pain are neither premeditated nor spiteful. It is easy to believe everyone is out to hurt me, when in fact most people are either unaware of my sorrow or honestly wanting to say and do the "right" things.

When telling others of our infertility, I have often heard, "I wish I had your problem," laughingly exclaimed by couples who have easily grown their families. In trying to explain fertility challenges to those who have never lived through such experiences, I have to remind myself that the outside perspective is one of innocence. My own perceptions were also much different before I walked this road. I try to remember times when I have hurt hearts with statements or actions that unintentionally inflicted pain.

While visiting my friend Julie shortly after her father's heart-related death, I shared a story about how surprised I had been over a certain incident. I flippantly used the figure of speech, "I just about had a heart attack," not only *once* in the course of that conversation, but *twice*. Each time I instantly wanted to chew off my own tongue for the poor choice of words, and yet I was so embarrassed that I just stumbled my way right on through my story, not even admitting to my insensitive tread on her tender feelings. Not knowing the right words to say, compounded by embarrassment over the words I had chosen, surely brought much pain to the friend I wanted only to encourage.

The stories I've heard are heartbreaking. Doctors suggest couples "scrap the whole thing" when talking to couples about their babies who are expected to be born with special needs or who threaten to come with preterm labor. Social workers ask potential adoptive parents when they plan to "buy" their babies. Pastors suggest that God's judgment is on bereaved parents or those unable to conceive. Loved ones place blame and admonish hurting families that they must not have "enough faith."

I could easily fill this book with nothing but words and actions that have brought pain. But because it is so easy to fall into a victim mentality, let's focus away from our personal discomfort for a moment and strive to understand the viewpoint of others. When someone is unkind, it may have much more to do with her daily battles than with my personal circumstances.

While we can see Hannah's misery recorded in the Bible, we don't know as much about Peninnah. I believe Peninnah had unfulfilled desires too. She wasn't just "the other woman"; she enjoyed all the legal, cultural, and traditional status that Hannah had as Elkanah's wife. Peninnah lived with a man who treated her well, but may not have wholeheartedly loved her. She was able to bear children, yet her fertility did not earn Peninnah first place in her husband's heart.

Maybe Peninnah turned her bitterness outward, much as I did with my yearning for motherhood. The barbs she tossed at Hannah may well have been thorns thrown in self-defense. Flaunting her fertility could have been the only way Peninnah knew how to cope with her own broken heart.

When my heart was grieved and my spirit embittered, I was senseless and ignorant; I was a brute beast before you.

PSALM 73:21-22

Putting Myself in My Friend's Shoes

One of my favorite stories is about an oyster complaining of the grain of sand in her shell. The tale describes the irritation this single, tiny speck causes for our oyster friend. Of course, when her life is over, where once there had been only dirt, now glows a priceless pearl.

My challenge, like Mrs. Oyster's, is to take the things that "get under my skin" and use them to God's glory. There are some things I can change, while for others I must seek the Lord's wisdom to endure my circumstances with grace. When my life is over, do I want to be remembered as that self-absorbed woman who could only focus on her own hurt, like Peninnah, or as a godly woman with a heart for others?

Before wallowing in my own misery, I can try to step back and evaluate a situation. When a friend says or does something that seems less than supportive, I can ask myself if there is anything in her life that is causing her frustration, and if so, how the Lord might want to use *me* to encourage her. If there is no apparent problem, I can still ask the Lord to help me love her in spite of the heartache she causes.

There are always going to be specific times (like when my hormones are a mess), places, or people that get under my skin, even when I try to seek the Lord's guidance. Granted, some days I am better at the Lord-love-her-through-me approach than others. But this strategy has saved me a lot of unneeded self-pity.

When I pray for those who cause me pain, sometimes God blesses me with unforeseen friendships I might otherwise never have known. That single mom, overwhelmed by her kids, may not have a clue about infertility, but if I prayerfully give her friendship a chance, I may be surprised at how deeply she understands loneliness and unfulfilled dreams from a different perspective.

Knowing that God is in control doesn't always keep pain at bay. As you find yourself in uncomfortable places or conversations, ask God to give you grace to survive the moment, along with an understanding heart to hear the *intended* meaning behind your friend's words.

When your friend says, "Don't you want to just trust God instead of taking those fertility drugs?" she may mean something more like "Reproductive medicine is a scary concept for me, and I would rather see God let you have a baby without you needing to endure any more grief." Or her suggestion to "just adopt and then you'll get pregnant" could be her way of expressing that she knows you are good motherhood material and she would like to see your arms filled as soon as possible.

Some of these conversations can be used as springboards for education. Ask the Lord to prepare your heart, even now, for ways to help your loved ones understand your needs. Prayerfully consider what you would like others to know about your grief, and when appropriate circumstances present themselves with friends who are open to listening, take time to lovingly explain how and why you are made uncomfortable by specific scenarios. Offer realistic suggestions (like those found in the "Burden Bearers" sections of each chapter) about how things could be handled more appropriately.

Let your conversation be always full of grace, seasoned with
salt, so that you may know how to answer everyone.

COLOSSIANS 4:6

For Further Thought

(From "Forgiving Cruel Remarks" by Ginger Garrett)

As Jesus hung on a cross, crucified by those who rejected Him as Savior, He
. . . spoke not a word of retaliation. Jesus did not attempt to justify Himself to
them or even try to respond to their insults with the truth. Instead, He spoke
forgiveness. "Father," He said, "forgive them, for they do not know what they
are doing." We may want to retaliate — but in fact, retaliating will only drive
others away at the very time we most need their prayers and encouragement.
Jesus calls us to forgive instead.

If you want to imitate Christ's example, you must forgive even before
you're asked. Also ask God to forgive the offender. Then try to lovingly
explain what words hurt and how friends and loved ones can best support
you. Many people simply don't know how to respond to suffering; forgiveness
frees you to guide them from hurting to helping.[1]

Heart Treasures

Genesis 29:9–30:24

Job 16:1-6

Psalm 88:8-9

Proverbs 12:16,18

Proverbs 14:10

Burden Bearers

Communication is imperative. You can have all the general guidelines in the world, but you can best minister to me by getting to know my heart and learning my triggers for rejoicing or heartache. When in doubt, ask me directly.

In some ways you are in a "no-win" situation. If you ignore me when it is time to send out baby shower invitations or birth announcements, it may make me feel all the more removed from normalcy. Yet if you do include me and I'm having an especially hard day, I may feel you have been insensitive. One idea might be to send me the same baby shower announcement that you are sending to all of our friends, but inside include a handwritten note acknowledging that you know this might bring me pain. Let me know that I am free to come or not, as I so desire, but that you love me and are praying for me.

Miriam wisely relates,

> My grief has made me vulnerable, thus sometimes I misunderstand what you say to me or take your words the wrong way. Please be patient with me. I do not want you to feel like you can't say anything to me or share from your heart, for I desire for you to talk to me and be my friend now more than ever! Please do not always wait for me to take initiative to get together and talk. I need you to be the one reaching out to me. It reassures me that you haven't stopped caring about me and still desire to be with me even when it is tough. And please, don't just assume things about me during this time of mourning. Ask me and let me share with you what I am learning.

If my baby has died, please *do* remember my child. Remember that I am a mother. Don't forget dates of significance, like my baby's due date or the anniversary of our loss.

If my miscarriage was "early," don't think my baby was any less a person, any less my child, any less significant, than if he had died later in life.

Don't tell me that my baby's death was probably "for the best." I know all about birth defects, better timing in my life, and so forth, but *my child is dead.* I know that somehow God can work even this for His good purpose, but right now I need you to validate my grief.

Make a point of calling my child by name when you are talking with me. While hearing my baby's name might bring tears to my eyes, it is music to my ears.

Above all, please keep me in your ongoing prayers. And every now and then, call me on the phone or drop a note in the mail just to remind me that you *are* praying.

(Please visit www.hannah.org/resources/friends.htm for additional resources.)

how long does it hurt?

This went on year after year. Whenever Hannah went up to
the house of the LORD, her rival provoked her till she wept and
would not eat.

1 SAMUEL 1:7

Then Jacob tore his clothes, put on sackcloth and mourned
for his son many days. All his sons and daughters came to
comfort him, but he refused to be comforted. "No," he said,
"in mourning will I go down to the grave to my son." So his
father wept for him.

GENESIS 37:34-35

*Culture dictated this time of feasting, yet Hannah found herself
observing an unplanned fast. Bitter, salty tears didn't mix well with
the food Elkanah lovingly provided. Why bother feeding a body that
had failed her, anyway? And as for her heart, did she really want it to
continue beating if it would only be an ongoing target for Peninnah's
brutality? Deeply depressed, she could nourish her spirit only with
tears. The very thought of food was repulsive.*

*Against her best intent, Hannah was learning the relentlessness
of mourning, the exhausting work of grief. She felt as though she
had been sent on an endless journey into the desert without a map.
Many months the oasis of hope hovered just beyond tangibility, only*

to dissolve like a mirage into the sand. Each time she thought she was
finally starting to feel a little better, something tripped her up again.
Would this parching thirst of her soul never end?

"I'm sick and tired of feeling sick and tired." These have been my words many times over the past fourteen years. A month before Rick and I met, the flu swept through campus, sending a vast majority of the student body to bed. While others were back on their feet within a few days, I just couldn't seem to get better.

For the first few weeks I figured I was just "run down" or "stressed," but surely would recover as soon as I could go home for a few days of Mom's cooking and my own bed. As time passed I became discouraged. I sat in the cafeteria, pushing food around my plate, unable to manage the overwhelming feat of taking a bite. "I can't believe I've been sick for six whole weeks!"

Added to constant fevers, pain, memory lapses, and exhaustion, I developed panic attacks and a host of phobias. I dropped out of school and moved back home. By then I was sleeping eighteen to twenty-three hours out of every twenty-four. I gave my mom more than one scare when I slept so deeply she feared I had stopped breathing. When I was coherent enough to give my situation any real thought, I vacillated between dismay and a sense of futility.

For seven months I played lab rat while doctors poked, prodded, and tested. The possibilities were often terrifying. After a while I stopped asking what they were looking for *this time.* I would rather not know what life-altering or life-threatening condition they next suspected until there was proof that I needed to worry. With each negative test result I felt simultaneous relief and frustration. "So glad it wasn't *that!* But why can't we find answers?"

I felt abandoned by many of my friends when it became apparent that my health would not quickly return. My life was suddenly so different. While I appreciated those who did attempt to help and encourage, I got weary of false hope repeatedly dangled before me as friends suggested diets, medications, treatments, herbal or natural remedies, jewelry to wear, prayers to pray, or other "sure cures."

At first I tried almost anything, sometimes resulting in deeper complications of my health conditions. I eventually became more skeptical and selective in what I investigated. I learned that I could not try every possible fix and that I needed to worry more about listening to God's leading for my life than about not wanting to hurt my friends' feelings.

By God's grace my parents' new insurance "randomly" assigned us to a Christian doctor who quickly and accurately diagnosed me with Chronic Fatigue Immune Dysfunction Syndrome. He came alongside me to teach me skills for managing and coping with a condition that is not fatal but will be a "thorn in my flesh" for as long as I live, unless God chooses to miraculously remove it.

There was given me a thorn in my flesh. . . . Three times I pleaded with the Lord to take it away from me. But he said to me, "My grace is sufficient for you, for my power is made perfect in weakness."

2 CORINTHIANS 12:7-9

What does chronic illness have to do with fertility challenges? Actually, the parallels are many. Normalcy invaded by medical exploration, a drive to find answers coupled with fear of what may be discovered, expectations colliding with reality, families and friendships tested, questioning of God, emotional ups and downs, and often a battle against depression.

"Everyday decisions" are no longer routine when living with a chronic illness. My health seems to impact every choice I make. When my grandmother suffered a stoke, I weighed the long-term physical consequences of attempting to travel back to be by her deathbed or attend her funeral against my emotional need for closure. I anguished over the options for days, but my body won out over my heart and I grudgingly chose not to travel. While my family understood and supported my decision, the weight of letting a disability dictate yet another major choice in my life was maddening.

Infertility provides many of the same decision crisis points: If we buy the larger home in hopes of filling it, will the empty rooms seem much too empty in the interim (or if they never do have inhabitants)? But if we buy smaller while knowingly trying to grow our family, might we regret such a decision very quickly, should children come sooner rather than later? Or can we even think of buying a house at all, when medical aid and adoption can be so costly?

The loss of a child brings even more quandaries. When a hoped-for adoption or early pregnancy is suddenly no more, do we tell the world or grieve in silence? When a child shared our home and heart, even for a brief time, how do we cope once she is gone? "Dare we try ever again, after having our hearts ripped out?" No one expects to need to make choices such as "Should we cremate or buy a burial plot?"

It can seem that all decisions either become rooted in or somehow always circle back to "the baby thing." *How can I get out of bed this morning, brush my teeth, and go through the motions of normal life when my life is anything but normal?* No matter how seemingly unrelated to my parenthood journey, anything that stirred up my emotions invariably led me back to my deepest pain: how much I missed our babies (and still do), how much I wanted to be a mommy to living children. I felt useless without being able to accomplish my one greatest goal in life. I felt lonely and unfulfilled. It all seemed so unfair.

Holidays and Anniversaries

When you read Hannah's story in its entirety, it becomes clear that, while Samuel was the answer to Hannah's prayers, *his* life was not an easy one. He was separated from his mother at a young age to live a life set apart, different from those around him. He saw his family only once a year, and then it was in the midst of a stressful, busy season of temple duties.

Sound anything like your own holiday traditions of travel and unrealistic expectations? Significant dates and events such as holidays are the landmarks that perhaps best capture the chronic nature of this grief. It is one thing to realize "it's been awhile" since you started trying to have a baby. It is another to think of all the birthdays, Thanksgivings, Christmases, and Mother's and Father's Days that are passing by. For the baby you have lost, there is the day you found out you were to become parents, your child's due date or birthday to survive each year, and the anniversary of the loss itself.

My twenty-fourth birthday was especially difficult. I had once heard that a woman is most fertile between the ages of sixteen and twenty-three, which is not much help to the vast majority of women who are not even married by then. (I realize many women easily achieve pregnancy well into their thirties or forties, but that knowledge did little to comfort my heart on this particular landmark.) In addition, my medical problems had indicated I might have to have a hysterectomy before my thirtieth birthday, and it seemed time was getting short. Friends offered consolation that I was "still young" and had "plenty of time," but their comfort was hollow.

The second Mother's Day after we set out to become parents was a nightmare. We had only recently learned that our first potential adoption lead would not end in our ability to bring two children into our family. I was feeling like a failure on every level: college dropout, chronically ill woman, partner in a business where I couldn't even lend my husband a hand, and unable to achieve something as "basic" as motherhood. At this point I truly wondered, *Of what value is my life?*

I started crying the moment all the mothers at church were invited to stand and receive a flower in honor of their motherhood status. I hardly stopped crying for the next three days. I spent that week in bed, using my health as a viable excuse. In reality I was deeply immersed in the grasp of depression. I refused to tend to personal hygiene. I ranted and raved and shook my fists at God. I tried to pray but felt heaven was deaf. I entertained thoughts of ending my life.

The emotions Mother's Days stirred within me were followed closely by many other major holidays. Father's Days, while they often seemed to go relatively unnoticed by Rick, left me again feeling like a failure, desperate to qualify my husband to receive a Tootsie Pop at church. Thanksgivings always seemed to have too few bodies gathered around our table, even in crowded, extended-family settings.

Birthdays and anniversaries marked the passing of years with unfulfilled goals and expectations. Even Labor Day, the day I was due to have been *in labor* with Noel, held a sting. Easters left me numb as I watched adorable children parade into church in their finest clothes while I struggled with a God who was not allowing me the opportunity to be a parent. At a time when everyone was celebrating the Resurrection, I took offense. As others saw hope, I was cloaked in grief. As they rejoiced in life, I focused on death. God Himself had a living Child, yet I was denied that.

I attended a ladies' party on our third childless Christmas. The pastor's wife, one of several pregnant women, gushed on and on about how being pregnant at Christmas made her feel such a kinship with Mary. My thought was "If even a *virgin* could give birth to a baby, I must really be in bad shape."

Do you realize how many Christmas carols include words such as *womb?* For many years I could not celebrate the Baby in the manger on any level, but had to fully focus my thanksgiving on the reason for His birth, that I might be reconciled to the Father through the death of the Son.

One Christmas I actually *was* pregnant, but didn't know in time for any Christmas morning excitement. Our baby's brief life was only confirmed after I began to miscarry. Now Christmas represented not only my inability to become a mother, but also the anniversary of our only child's death.

While the due dates of each of my miscarried babies have been hard, I've found the days or weeks leading up to these significant landmarks to be more difficult than the days themselves. There is a growing dread as the date approaches, a fear that I might suffocate if it gets any harder.

Then the landmark itself is upon me. And yes, it is painful, but sometimes almost anticlimactic after all the dreadful anticipation. If you are fearful of an upcoming date, take heart that you truly can survive.

When times are good, be happy; but when times are bad,
consider: God has made the one as well as the other.

ECCLESIASTES 7:14

The Return of Laughter

The loss of a child, either a unique individual or the child who will never be though he has filled your hopes and dreams of a lifetime, is not something you ever fully "get over." Just as Jacob, after being told of his son's death, could not imagine life ever again without tears, you may be in the darkest days of grief right now. *How long will it hurt?* In some sense, forever.

Physically, I lead a "new normal" life now, no longer bedridden, but carefully weighing each activity so as not to tip the scales precariously into relapse. There are times I think I'm doing well, then suddenly I'm back in bed for a few days (or more). I can never go back to the way things were, but I can find fulfillment in my new reality.

Grief ebbs and flows much the same way. Both my illness and my infertility are constantly there, a part of my makeup, but at times one or the other may push to the forefront and demand my attention. But more often now they each simply exist without fully defining me.

With time and by the Lord's grace, there will come a day when you surprise yourself by hearing your own laughter again. "Even in laughter the heart may ache" (Proverbs 14:13), but when that day comes, there is no need to feel guilt in experiencing moments of joy.

I will turn their mourning into gladness; I will give them
comfort and joy instead of sorrow.

JEREMIAH 31:13

For Further Thought

A few of the warning signs of depression include dramatic changes in eating or sleeping habits or sexual drive. Other signs are persistent feelings of intense sadness, anger, or indifference. While often triggered or intensified by emotional issues, depression often has a medical component. Depression is *not* a sign of weakness or spiritual failure. The psalms are filled with words written from great depths of despair. Please do not be afraid to reach out and seek aid from a friend, your pastor, a Christian counselor, or your doctor. If you seek support only to be told, "Chin up!" or "Snap out of it," look elsewhere for help.

Many women face a double whammy of managing both chronic illness and fertility challenges. Lisa Copen, adoptive mother and founder of Rest Ministries (www.restministries.org), understands both of these struggles very personally. Be sure to explore her resources for both infertility and for making the painful choice not to pursue parenthood due to health limitations. Here you will find great, Christ-centered encouragement for living daily with pain or illness.

Heart Treasures

Psalm 102:4-9

Ecclesiastes 3:1-4

2 Corinthians 12:7-10

Burden Bearers

My friend Beth shares,

> Although my husband suffers from many severe and painful health problems, I would never say that I *understand* what he's going through. I understand from my perspective, but I am not the one up and down all night, dealing with chronic pain and constantly having to be medicated just to function like a normal person. I would never belittle his problems and his pain by saying, "I know exactly what you are going through." It hurts to have someone who has never been treated like a pin cushion, had the privacy and intimacy of her marriage exposed, been through the ups and downs of hormone therapies, had surgery or been on the roller coaster of trying-to-conceive emotions, belittle my pain with such statements.

There may be times I need to opt out of family gatherings. Reunions, watching your kids rip open packages under the tree on Christmas morning, baby dedications, your child's birthday party — any of these may be too fresh a reminder of the reality that may never be mine.

Please let me know of resources that might help me. If you hear of a local support group, another couple with whom we could talk and fellowship, a caring pastor who would listen with a tender heart, please tell me. But once you have shared your resources, please don't push me. Pray that I will be ready to seek this help when God's timing is right for me to do so.

If you see signs of suicidal tendencies in my words or actions, do not hesitate in getting me professional help immediately. Our community or church likely has a crisis number where you can seek assistance. (Worldwide suicide prevention phone numbers are listed at www.suicide-helplines.org.)

two hearts beating as one … sometimes

Elkanah her husband would say to her, "Hannah, why are you weeping? Why don't you eat? Why are you downhearted? Don't I mean more to you than ten sons?"

1 Samuel 1:8

For this reason a man will leave his father and mother and be united to his wife, and they will become one flesh.

Genesis 2:24

Elkanah was exasperated to find her crying yet again. No doubt, she and Peninnah had just had another spat. Their rivalry was tiresome, but what bothered him most was his inability to provide Hannah with the one thing that would erase her misery. Whenever she got like this, he felt like such a failure. 'Is it the baby thing again? We've talked about this before. I would give you children if I could, but it's out of our hands.'

It was a devastating blow to realize that his love alone would never be enough to fully comfort his precious bride. "We have each other and that's what's really important anyway. I married you for you!" He had tried so many things to bring her joy, but nothing seemed to help. Maybe if he could just get some food down her she would feel better.

As he piled her plate with a double portion of the choicest selections from the banquet, he prayed that the way to this woman's heart might be through her stomach.

One of the biggest challenges we face in our journey through infertility is maintaining the unity in our marriage. I've written this chapter to be read by both husbands and wives, and I've tried to cover a variety of issues that can cause marital disharmony in this difficult time.

It is rare for couples to experience emotions in unison. I often hear, "My husband says that if God wants us to have a baby, He will make it happen when the time is right. He has such peace, and it's driving me crazy!" Rick was the one who initially came to *me* with the desire to have a baby, so I couldn't understand why I was the one who seemed so driven to get pregnant and frustrated when it didn't happen.

For Rick, there were times to focus on the heartache and longing, and times to turn our attention to other parts of life. He could analyze and compartmentalize while my every thought was consumed with the desire for motherhood. We would go to a ball game and he would passionately cheer for the team or shout instructions to the coaches. I would sit in the bleachers and count the little children in attendance.

Unlike my husband, I found that infertility defined me. Someone would ask, "What do you do?" and Rick would answer with a description about his job, while I hoped no one would aim the same question my direction. "Stay-at-home mom" was a socially acceptable answer. "Stay-at-home *non*-mom" never went over so well. I used the code word *homemaker*, but figured everyone could see through my disguise.

Sometimes it feels like your partner is sleeping through a crisis. He may never seem to take the struggle of infertility as seriously as you do. A failed adoption or your baby's death can be like being caught in a burning house. The two of you run in different directions, tripping into and over each other, trying to escape the terror. As the suffocating heat closes around you, part of the panic comes from lack of assurance that you are still together in this darkness. It is easy to fall into the trap of believing that there is only one *right* way to grieve — "my way."

Submission — Even in Grief?

While their barrenness was beyond the control of either Elkanah or Hannah, God ordained Elkanah to guide his family through the process. The apostle Paul gives this admonition: "Wives, submit to your husbands as to the Lord. For the husband is the head of the wife as Christ is the head of the church, his body, of which he is the Savior. Now as the church submits to Christ, so also wives should submit to their husbands in everything" (Ephesians 5:22-24).

Ladies, I know red flags start going up here. *Submission* can be an unsettling concept. Since sin first entered the world with Adam and Eve, it's been hard to let men lead. We know, from heart experience, that one of the results of Eve's sin was pain related to childbearing. But what was the other part of Eve's curse?

As a direct result of our sin nature, we have an impulsive drive to run the show. Though Genesis 3:16 is usually translated as a woman's desire being *for* or *toward* her husband, many Bible scholars believe *against* to be the intended contextual and linguistic application of the conjunctive. While my desires often conflict with Rick's, God set him in authority over our family. I'm still learning that I need to trust Rick and let the Lord lead our family through him.

If you are married to a man who is not striving to live for God, seek the Lord's guidance to find the balance between submitting to your husband's wishes and making God-honoring decisions. Your attitude toward your groom may become the very tool God uses to lead your husband closer to Himself.

When married to a man, Christian or not, who is pushing you to do something immoral (perhaps insisting on an abortion because of your baby's birth defect), clearly and lovingly share your concerns. If he is open to Scripture, show him directly from the Word of God why you are troubled by what he is asking of you. When it comes down to a choice, you must obey God rather than man (see Peter's story in Acts 4).

Presuming you aren't being asked to participate in anything morally objectionable, it is imperative to consult with your husband before you commit to anything that will impact your family and future together. When my doctor presents a medical course that offers me hope, it is hard to hold back when Rick gives a flat-out no, or even when he wants to just take time to prayerfully seek more answers. But my marriage vows are to my husband, not to my doctor or anyone else.

> *For this is the way the holy women of the past who put their hope in God used to make themselves beautiful. They were submissive to their own husband, like Sarah, who obeyed Abraham. . . . You are her daughters if you do what is right and do not give way to fear.*
>
> 1 PETER 3:5-6

I can point to definite times when, had I given Rick's concerns more credence, I would have saved us both a lot of heartache. An example that immediately comes to mind is the adoption lead I pushed hard to pursue, even when Rick repeatedly, though quietly, stated his discomfort with certain aspects of the situation. It turned out to be a scam. I could have prevented much grief by listening to Rick's misgivings early on.

In the very week I am writing this chapter, I've spoken with three women about regrets over past choices in their fertility journeys. These were choices they pushed for that will carry lifelong painful consequences. In each of these cases the husband had mentioned some level of concern with the given pursuit, while the wife felt it to be the "right thing." Each woman longs to be able to turn back time and give her husband's comments more prayerful consideration. Here's one such example:

I didn't realize how much having a child had consumed my life. It's so easy for women to take the lead in managing the infertility situation.

My husband wanted to please me, and I think some things he went along with because he wanted to make me happy. . . . I realize now that I wasn't being submissive.

He still needs to be the leader in my family, and he still needs to be part of the decision-making process. There are so many decisions to make. We've been struggling with infertility for over three years, so it's not like we rushed into our decision. But with his personality, I think he was afraid to make the decisions, so he let me take the lead.

Does this mean our husband's decisions are always the "correct" ones? Not necessarily. But we are called to trust God by allowing our husbands to lead us, even in the face of their very human fallibility.

Wives, I challenge you to allow your husband to take the leadership role God has given him. If he doesn't guide your family in this process, resist the temptation to make all the decisions, but gently encourage your husband to help you with them.

Actively pursuing family growth is *not* sinful. But an obsessive drive that rushes you ahead of God's leading is. If God is convicting your husband about something while striving to build your family, be open to hearing his concerns. Your husband is treating you with honor and love when he is honest with you. The Bible is clear that your marital relationship is to be a gentle, loving partnership in order to maintain clear communication with God.

While yielding to conviction is imperative, it is also important to note that just because something seems unnatural or uncomfortable, it isn't necessarily outside God's plan for your family. One of you may be ready to apply to an adoption agency long before the other is even ready to consider the possibility. One might not feel any peace about taking another step down the medical route, while the other wants to go as far as humanly possible in pursuit of a biological child.

The marriage passage in Ephesians 5 actually starts with instructions to all Christians: "Submit to one another out of reverence for Christ" (verse 21). Many times the concept of "mutual submission" is overlooked within marriage, but we need to remember that our spouse is also our brother or sister in the Lord. Take time to truly hear what your spouse is thinking, and give fair and prayerful consideration to all the feelings and desires.

Husbands, leading your wife in a godly and loving marriage is a weighty responsibility. Because you love her, you must seek hard after God's best and make wise decisions together with her. Carefully research the options and bathe each choice in prayer. Where either of your hearts or bodies are involved, do not unilaterally mandate the course you will follow.

Putting Your Husband First

In the struggle to "have a family," it can be so easy to forget that as husband and wife we already are a family. It is important never to lose sight of this fact. The woman I quoted on the submission issue above continues:

> I realized that in my own struggles with infertility, I had neglected my husband's needs. When we give all our time and attention to infertility, our husbands can get lost in the shuffle. I never realized how much I was focusing on the infertility and not on my husband. Our conversations, our time, our money — everything — related to infertility. My husband should have been my top priority, but he wasn't. I wish I had a nickel for every infertility comment I made when I could have been complimenting my husband or building him up.

What most attracted you to your spouse in the beginning? Why did you marry? What do you most admire about your partner? What joint activities bring you the most shared pleasure? If these answers don't readily spring to mind, it has been too long since you shared a common heartbeat. Sit down and list your answers on paper, then pursue ways to add to your lists of joys together.

Keep the Bedroom Stress-Free

How's your sex life? Yes, I know, it is a blunt question. The sexual relationship is a common area of conflict in many marriages, along with issues such as money and time usage. Whatever your "issues" prior to infertility or the loss of a child, they are almost always intensified through this journey. Sometimes things that were fine before have now become problematic. I've heard from more than one couple that their sexual frustrations (embarrassment over "performance" due to the stress of timed intercourse; fears and grief tied to the marriage act because of its tie to conception; extreme imbalance of sex drives between spouses) are actually *more* painful than infertility itself.

I've known couples at every point in the spectrum, from "My wife will only let me have sex with her when she is ovulating" to "Make love three times a day, every day, for ninety days and if that doesn't do it, there's no hope for pregnancy." Neither of these are exceptionally healthy attitudes nor medically the best methods for conception. Talk to your doctor about the optimum timing for your specific situation.

However, the "optimum" for your given medical scenario must be weighed against biblical guidelines and the desire to minister to your partner. Yes, there are certain variances that must be made when pursing fertility treatments, but when doctor-prescribed timing continually eclipses marital enjoyment, there's a problem. Husbands frequently report frustration because their wives seem uninterested in sex all month long, then suddenly become aggressive in the bedroom only when ovulation time comes. These guys want to be pursued for more than just their sperm!

Some couples confess to embarrassment (and often dishonesty in their answers) during fertility evaluations when their doctors question sexual frequency. The emotional expense of fertility challenges can easily account for some desire imbalances between husband and wife or low desire in both partners. According to the developer of DivorceBusting.com, "low sexual desire isn't only a 'woman's thing.' Many sex experts believe that low sexual desire in a man is America's best kept secret."[1] Wives often have the significantly stronger desire for sexual intimacy. When their efforts to seduce their husbands (as advised in almost any marriage resource on the topic) are repeatedly rebuffed, these women are left feeling rejected, hurt, and undesirable.

Causes of infertility, such as low testosterone production in men or overproduction of the same hormone in women, may play a factor too. Some husbands intentionally hold back every month during the two weeks post-ovulation (and longer, if pregnancy is then confirmed), in fear of causing the anguish of miscarriage.

God intended the marriage bed not only for procreation and for pleasure, but also for comfort (see Genesis 24:67 and 2 Samuel 12:24). Do your best to keep your bedroom a safe haven of refuge from the stresses of fertility challenges. While the desperation might make it feel otherwise, your marriage relationship truly must remain a higher priority than having babies. What good is it to bring children into your family when your marriage is falling apart as a result of the quest?

With or without children, strive to bless one another.

For Further Thought

Wives, are there areas where you are taking a leadership role without listening to your husband's insights? Ask the Lord to help you put your journey to parenthood under His authority, through submission to your husband.

Husbands, are you regularly expressing your love and support to your wife during this time of heartache? Ask the Lord to show you creative ways to treat your bride with honor and to work with her in godly decision-making processes.

Heart Treasures

Genesis 3

Judges 13

Proverbs 27:15-16

1 Corinthians 7

Ephesians 5:22-33

1 Peter 3:1-7

Burden Bearers

Sexual tensions often run high during infertility. After the death of a baby, physical intimacy is emotionally entangled with the creation (and loss) of life. Statements such as "Do you guys know how babies are made?" or "At least you can have fun trying!" cut me to the core.

Please pray for every aspect of our marriage to be strengthened through this time of trial. Send us on a date night (a dinner gift certificate, a packed picnic basket, an offer to babysit our living children), or give us resources to strengthen our marriage (tickets to a marriage conference, a subscription to a Christian couples' magazine, marriage devotional books).

fill my cup, Lord

Once when they had finished eating and drinking in Shiloh,
Hannah stood up. Now Eli the priest was sitting on a chair by
the doorposts of the LORD's temple.

1 SAMUEL 1:9

Although the Lord gives you the bread of adversity and the
water of affliction . . . Whether you turn to the right or to the
left, your ears will hear a voice behind you, saying, "This is the
way; walk in it."

ISAIAH 30:20-21

*She desperately tried to choke down a few bites just to make Elkanah
happy, but swallowing past the hard knot in her throat was nearly
impossible. What a relief when the joyless feast was finally over! Weary
from the battle, eyes puffy, and head pounding, Hannah struggled to
her feet. What should they do now? Where could she turn?*

*Overwhelmed by the longing to cradle a child in her arms, Hannah's
mind turned toward memories of her own childhood and the stories
heard at her mother's knee. The name Jehovah Jireh, praising God as
Provider, whispered quietly through her aching heart. Could He truly
provide answers for someone like her?*

*Though yet buried under callused layers of bitter grief, this
question ignited the first fragile spark of hope her heart had known*

*in many years. Hannah's trembling legs carried her to the house of the
Lord with strength she had not known she possessed. While Hannah
had never doubted the faith of her youth, today she would step out in
this faith as never before, determined to find peace.*

I equate Hannah's flight to the temple with my own quest for answers. *Why,
Lord? I don't understand. Don't You see how my heart is breaking? Are You here?
Do you care? Why is it so easy for some and so hard for us? Does my faith affect
Your plans? What if I just pray harder? Is medical aid allowable? If so, how far
can we go with science? What about adoption? Where will the money come
from? Why does this have to hurt so much?*

While I gave my all in the pursuit of parenthood, my methods always
seemed to fall short. God had the final say and I felt like a puppet on a string,
at His mercy, performing without a script. In my quest for answers, I came
face to face with the bitter reality that I wanted to let God be my Lord only
as long as He did things on my terms.

We had been blindly rushing from discouraging doctor's appointment
to dead-end adoption lead, becoming frustrated with financial roadblocks
along the way, for far too long. Sure we had been praying, "Lord, please give
us a baby," but we hadn't made His plan the focus of our quest. We honestly
hadn't even considered our need for such a focus — parenthood was just
supposed to happen!

Hannah's act of standing signifies her realization that she could not find
answers alone. She knew where to go with her questions. My turning point,
like Hannah's, came when I tearfully raised my arms to the Lord, like a child
waiting to be lifted by my Father. By sacrificially unclenching my grasp on all
my fears and stresses, asking in return for wisdom as we faced our dizzying
array of choices, I was consciously stepping back to really listen for His voice
in the quietness of my heart. In turning toward the temple with her broken
dreams, I believe Hannah was beginning to realize the same pain and peace
in letting go of her illusions of control.

Can We Trust God?

Stories of God's faithfulness were taught to Israelite children from the cradle, so His trustworthiness was not a foreign concept to Hannah. In seeking God's plan for her future, she needed only to look to history for reassurance that He was in control. We, being of the "new order" under grace, have even more evidence that God does not abandon those He loves. And yet fertility challenges can easily leave us feeling deserted by God. Head knowledge doesn't always spawn heart-deep faith.

Behind the curtain of the tabernacle, where Hannah sat in prayer, stood the ark of the covenant. Here was contained a jar of manna, a reminder of the time when Hannah's ancestors fled Egyptian slavery. God used Moses to lead this great nation into the wilderness, yet they quickly succumbed to the-grass-is-greener syndrome, saying, "If only we had died by the Lord's hand in Egypt! There we sat around pots of meat and ate all the food we wanted, but you have brought us out into this desert to starve this entire assembly to death" (Exodus 16:3).

God had every right to burn with anger against His ungrateful chosen nation. And yet He showed patience and compassion in the face of their whining. Rather than fire and brimstone, he rained down bread from heaven to fill their stomachs and strengthen their hearts. As their journey continued, He brought water gushing from solid rock — twice — to meet the thirst of this great nation of wilderness wanderers.

The Lord provided just enough sweet manna for the daily needs of each family. It could not be hoarded or stored without spoiling. In the same way, when Jesus taught His disciples to pray, he instructed them to ask for *daily bread*. I cannot stock up on God's grace, but must daily seek Him.

Just as I need to keep my physical body hydrated, I need to drink continually of Living Water, being careful to seek strength from a pure source, not from counterfeit wells. As I thirst for righteousness and meet this need at the feet of Jesus, my heart learns to listen for His still, small voice. I want my appetite to be appeased by "every word that comes from the mouth of the LORD" (Deuteronomy 8:3).

God's Holy Spirit took up residence within my soul the day I accepted the forgiveness of my sins. I became irrevocably adopted into God's family. And yet I am commanded to strive continually to have my heart transformed into His image. To be filled with the Holy Spirit is an ongoing process rather than a one-time act.

While my broken heart may leave me feeling abandoned by God, I have assurance that He is always with me, even when I go through seasons of spiritual drought. It is easy to get so caught up in my disillusionment that I miss out on the best God wants for me *today*. "Seek first his kingdom and his righteousness. . . . Therefore do not worry about tomorrow, for tomorrow will worry about itself. Each day has enough trouble of its own" (Matthew 6:33-34).

Seek first his kingdom . . . that was the key. I had to surrender and admit I didn't have the answers, seeking His instead. I had to commit to truly listening for His voice as I spent time in Scripture and prayer each day. I had to ask Him to show me His will — and really mean it. As I gradually opened my heart to what He might want for me, I began to have more peace than I'd experienced since my infertility journey began.

More Than I Could Ever Want

Remember the woman at the well? She couldn't handle the looks and whispers, so she came in the middle of the day to avoid the rest of the town's women, who would be there morning and evening. Looking to fill the void in her heart, she had been wed five times and was living with a man outside the bonds of marriage. Then suddenly this great man, a Jew, rumored to be a prophet, met her in her place of disgrace.

Jesus humbled Himself to ask her for a drink of water, then offered the quenching of her soul's thirst. The Greek phrase translated *living water* in John 4:10-11 is closely related to the Ephesians concept of being filled with the Holy Spirit (see Ephesians 5:18).

"I have come that they may have life, and have it to the full."

JOHN 10:10

She sought happiness in the arms of men. Jesus provides peace that could be found in none other than Himself.

I sought joy in the new life of a baby. Jesus offers New Life in Himself.

I wanted to know the feeling of carrying another soul inside my body. He provides the Holy Spirit to indwell me.

I longed to nurse a child. Paul wrote, "Like newborn babies, crave pure spiritual milk, so that by it you may grow up in your salvation, now that you have tasted that the Lord is good" (1 Peter 2:2-3).

I dreamed of watching my baby grow and mature. But am *I* ever-growing in Christ? "Anyone who lives on milk, being still an infant, is not acquainted with the teaching about righteousness. But solid food is for the mature, who by constant use have trained themselves to distinguish good from evil" (Hebrews 5:13-14).

I bemoaned the "bread of adversity" I felt unfairly called to taste. The Lord answers with the cross: "And he took bread, gave thanks and broke it, and gave it to them, saying, 'This is my body given for you; do this in remembrance of me'" (Luke 22:19).

I pleaded for a child to enrich my days on earth. He commands, "But store up for yourselves treasures in heaven, where moth and rust do not destroy, and where thieves do not break in and steal. For where your treasure is, there your heart will be also" (Matthew 6:20-21).

On the last and greatest day of the Feast, Jesus stood and said in a loud voice, "If anyone is thirsty, let him come to me and drink. Whoever believes in me, as the Scripture has said, streams of living water will flow from within him."

JOHN 7:37-38

For Further Thought

A dozen years ago I began chronicling significant life-lessons God was teaching me. I sometimes go months without picking up my pen, while my thoughts beg to be written daily during other seasons. Some entries are two or three words long, while a few fill dozens of pages.

Several handwritten volumes now line the top shelf of my bookcase. In seasons when the Lord seems silent to my cries, I can pull down my journals and am reminded that He has never forsaken me in dark places. A conscious choice to remember God's faithfulness in past circumstances eases my feelings of abandonment.

If you don't have a recorded history for revisiting God's workings in your life, this journey through heartache is a great place to start keeping track. Be as formal or informal as you'd like. Use a notebook, scraps of paper, your computer, even the margins of this book. Don't worry about writing skills, because this document is between only you and the Lord. Just record your heart in whatever form will be meaningful to you in the future.

You might begin by listing times God has proved Himself real to you, asking Him to bring to mind those you have forgotten. Then move into your struggles of today. Be brutally honest with God, telling Him of your anger, fears, frustrations, hopes, and dreams. Use this tool as you read the next few chapters of this book and see how the Lord clarifies to you His desires for your life. A year, six months, maybe even just a few weeks from now, look back and see what God has done in your heart through the process of recording your prayers.

Heart Treasures

Exodus 16–17

Exodus 25:23-30

Psalm 27:8

Psalm 114:8

Isaiah 49:10

Matthew 6:9-21

Matthew 15:11-20

John 4:4-26

John 6 (Look for every use of the word *bread*.)

Hebrews 9

Burden Bearers

If you were to eat rotten food, you would soon be on your knees from the abdominal pain of food poisoning. As I writhe under the cramping of my soul, it is the bitter cup of affliction and stale bread of adversity that drive me to my knees in anguished prayer. In the midst of pain, my focus may seem terribly self-centered. Please keep praying for me that I may clearly hear God's still, small voice comforting and guiding me through this process.

bitterness of soul

In bitterness of soul Hannah wept much
and prayed to the LORD.

1 SAMUEL 1:10

Therefore I will not keep silent;
I will speak out in the anguish of my spirit,
I will complain in the bitterness of my soul.

JOB 7:11

She had made it to the courts of the tabernacle. In this holy place would El Shaddai, God Almighty, listen to the humble cries of a simple, broken woman?

As she opened her mouth to utter her first words of praise and petition, she found herself mute, overcome with tears like none she had ever known. Her body shook with the sobbing. The floodgates of her heavy heart had fully burst under the strain.

There was no stopping the flow. Her sorrow was now the only gift she had to bring. She would be real before her Lord. The cleansing gush must be allowed to sweep away so many years of built-up tension. Could God find this offering of tears pleasing? Would He meet her in this place of anguish?

As month after month, then year after year, passed without the blessing of a living child in our home, my soul learned the foul taste of bitterness. My angry, festering heart ached constantly. That Hannah "wept much" seems to be a terribly inadequate description for the torrent of tears that accompanied me through years of longing and loss.

Though bitterness does not necessarily *represent* anger, it does seem to readily *accompany* anger. Anger, while a legitimate stage in coping with such life-shattering events as infertility or the loss of a child, can easily lead into bitterness if I allow it to remain in my life long term. God does not forbid the emotion of anger, but He does give careful guidelines about how I must handle it. The goal is to get through this angry state without letting bitterness take hold of my heart.

When my first nephew was a couple of years old, I had a feeling it wouldn't be long before my brother and his wife would be ready for their second. I decided to be proactive in coping with the sting of the announcement, so I asked my mom to ask them *not* to call me when another baby was on the way. I wanted to be informed by a family friend who was close enough to all of us that she would be both very excited for Dan and Diana and understanding of my need to vent my grief before I could be prepared to rejoice.

Receiving the news from Susan would allow me to process all the emotions I needed to work through without worrying about causing pain to my family. I could then pick up the phone and sincerely share in the celebration without feeling so broken. By clearly communicated my "rules" for receiving the news, I stopped dwelling on when or how I might be blindsided. So when my parents went to visit my brother, it didn't even occur to me that this would be "the time," until my mom called to say my sister-in-law was pregnant but on her way to the hospital because of bleeding.

You would think, after my own experience with miscarriage and as the head of a pregnancy loss support ministry, I would have dropped to my knees in prayer for Diana and the baby. Instead anger reared its ugly head, and the venom of bitterness shot deep into my heart. Sobbing, I called

Susan, not out of concern for my nephew's life, but to complain about how I had been mistreated. I was so mad that my family hadn't respected my very specific request, I really struggled to even pray because I felt my toes had been so stepped on. I know that sounds ridiculously petty, and I'm embarrassed about my behavior. But it sure gives me a clear picture of how deeply bitterness had invaded my heart.

Bitterness in the Bible

As my dreams of motherhood tarnished, I fell into a deep, black hole of anger at God. I felt so useless. Rachel knew this feeling of utter despair. She demanded of Jacob, "Give me children, or I'll die!" (Genesis 30:1). He replied that God was the One she needed to be talking to. Perhaps Jacob was angry, not only with Rachel, but with God as well.

Because they too were human, many biblical role models succumbed to the devastation of bitterness of soul when faced with painful situations. While I do not have the room to highlight each one, I would like to look at a few stories with you. These give us a better understanding of bitterness from God's point of view.

Jeremiah spouts deep bitterness of the soul as he laments the destruction of Jerusalem and the suffering of his people: "I remember my affliction and my wandering, the bitterness and the gall. I well remember them, and my soul is downcast within me" (Lamentations 3:19-20). The phrase "bitterness and gall" has a certain ring to it. What is gall anyway? It is a nasty, greenish-yellow fluid secreted by the liver and stored in the gallbladder to aid in the digestion of food. It is a very bitter, acidic substance, designed to break down and destroy. It's that burning, bitter taste in your mouth after you have vomited. To hear Jeremiah describe bitterness of the soul as being equal to gall begins to paint a clearer picture of what the pain of fertility challenges can be like when we allow bitterness to take root in our hearts.

King David must have been tempted toward embittered anger — if not directed toward God, then certainly toward himself. His infant son was ill as a result of his own sin. (This was before Christ brought us under grace. Please read chapter 3 for more information about sin in relationship to fertility challenges.) David pleaded with God and refused to eat for an entire week, devoting himself to prayer. He must have poured out great bitterness during those hours and days as he advocated for mercy on his son's behalf.

Naomi knew the pain of a bitter heart too. She lost her husband and both sons in a foreign country. When she returned home with only one faithful daughter-in-law, Naomi's soul was so wounded that when her friends called her Naomi, a name that means "pleasant," she replied, "Call me Mara, because the Almighty has made my life very bitter. I went away full, but the LORD has brought me back empty" (Ruth 1:20-21). Literally translated, the Hebrew word *mara* means "bitter." The idea behind this word is marrow, or the core substance of something; thus Naomi's bitterness penetrated through the very depths of her being.

Mara is quite similar to the word used to describe the bitterness Hannah faced as she went before God after years of pain and longing for a child. Hannah's bitterness, *marah,* also indicated great heaviness, disconnection, and chafing.

Bitterness is described in Hebrews as a root that defiles the soul, causing us to miss the grace of God. Nothing chokes out peace faster. Intense *marah* was deeply rooted within my heart for a long time. I felt raw, weighed down, constantly rubbed in the wrong direction. I was disconnected from God, my husband, my friends, and even myself.

God's Slow Surgery

I hadn't intended to let bitterness grow within my heart, but I hadn't actively prevented it either. Like a garden that is not weeded, a soul that is not continually refreshed and challenged by the Word of God and the work of the Holy Spirit becomes ready ground for bitterness to spring forth. Bitterness had been growing for a long time before I fully realized this weed's existence within me, and once discovered, it was already so strong I wasn't sure I wanted to give it up.

Allowing bitterness to dampen my relationship with the Lord invited the very neglect that embittered me. I put up a solid wall around the garden of my heart, breaking fellowship with God. By not allowing the Gardener access to tend the soil, I forfeited the peace He yearned to bring. Beginning with one tiny shoot, my heart was devoured by ugly roots of hurt and self-pity.

I felt totally neglected and abandoned. I figured if God really loved me, He would not deny this natural desire for motherhood that He had created within me. How could I trust a God who would play such a cruel game, to fashion me with an incredibly strong drive to reproduce then not enable me to accomplish that task of becoming a parent?

Going to God, I often felt I was beating my head against a wall (perhaps the one I had built?). While I never experienced a time of doubting His existence, I really wondered if He actually heard my prayers, for heaven seemed to echo them back in my face without answer. Loneliness, anger, and bitterness fed each other in a vicious cycle.

I was much like a child who had fallen and scraped my knee. My Father yearned to tend the wound, but rather than leaning into His strong arms, I struggled and pushed Him away. My kicking and fighting not only prevented the beginning of healing, but also caused much deeper pain in the process.

The more hurt I felt, the more I blamed the Lord for my pain. As my anger reached an irrational level, I hit one of the lowest points in my life. All of the waiting, disappointment, frustration, faith, hope, prayer, begging, pleading, doctors' visits, and medication seemed futile. God seemed so very far away.

Finally I had it out with God in a yelling, stomping, fist-shaking, tearful fit unlike any I had ever dared before. As a "good Christian" I had never fully admitted to Him, or to myself, just how angry I really was. But He had known the true nature of my heart all along.

I couldn't shock or surprise Him with my temper tantrum. He was big enough to handle all my rage. By confronting Him, I admitted to both of us exactly how I perceived our relationship. But this didn't drive Him further away; He drew me close. Honesty unlocked the rusty gate to that wall around my heart.

The truth is, even when He *seems* silent to my cries, He is listening and does care, grieving deeply with me in my loneliness. Not only does He care, but He also relates with personal understanding. Remember Jesus' cry from the cross, "My God, why have you forsaken me"?

I hadn't cared that I was causing my Father pain by locking Him out of my life. While I demanded the joy of motherhood, I never stopped to consider how it would break my heart to be rejected by my child in the way I was treating the Lord. By grace, just as I would never stop loving a prodigal, God's persistent love never abandoned me either.

But neither did His love trespass where uninvited. In order for fellowship to be restored, I had to ask Him to knock down walls and weed my heart.

If it is time to sacrifice your broken spirit to the Lord, I must offer you a word of caution. It can be difficult to face a bitter soul and deal with the core issues that drive prolonged anger. Remember the long process that first allowed this root to spread through your soul. Do not become discouraged when you go to God and are not immediately "all better" from your pain.

God often performs a slow surgery to gently release His children from the snarled fingers of destructive anger and the ugly grasp of bitterness. Don't give up on His healing touch, but keep trying to pray, even if your only prayers are yelled at God in total disillusionment. Keep taking your pain to God. He cannot help you if you lock Him out, hide, or run away. Be honest with Him and don't hold back.

Jesus declares, "I am the true vine, and my Father is the gardener. He cuts off every branch in me that bears no fruit, while every branch that does bear fruit he prunes so that it will be even more fruitful" (John 15:1-2). Pruning often seems even more painful than letting bitterness remain rooted, but God is the master Gardener who desires to see you bloom. By drinking deeply of Living Water, even when you don't feel like it, the soil of your heart will slowly soften, allowing the weeds to less painfully release their hold on your heart.

Preventing bitterness from again rooting requires daily vigilance. The process of turning my heartache over to God used to be a moment-by-moment, breath-by-breath endeavor. By God's great grace, I have been freed from the stranglehold of *marah* long enough that it is now a matter of ongoing weeding as painful situations arise. Whenever I start to let anger control my heart, I must recommit my bitterness triggers to the Lord.

God has a plan that is better than anything I can imagine. He knows the ultimate purpose of each ingredient He allows to flavor my life. As bitter as His recipe may seem, God can make it good, accomplishing His great purpose.

"For I know the plans I have for you," declares the Lord, *"plans to prosper you and not to harm you, plans to give you hope and a future. Then you will call upon me and come and pray to me, and I will listen to you. You will seek me and find me when you seek me with all your heart."*

JEREMIAH 29:11-13

For Further Thought

Are you caught in the trap of *marah* bitterness that brought Hannah to her knees? If so, what steps do you need to take in asking God to remove the pain? If not, how can you actively prevent such bitterness from rooting in your heart?

You may not feel God's presence at the moment, but He is here. He has been with you through all your pain. He longs to forgive your sinful anger, to soothe away your bitterness, and to comfort your soul, just as you would long to comfort the child for whom you grieve. You are free to weep with Hannah in your pain, but that bitter weeping must be done *before the Lord*. By continually seeking Him in prayer, bitterness will have no soil in which to take root. God's grace will abound when the roadblocks to that grace are removed.

Heart Treasures

Deuteronomy 29:18 (Could a baby be a god in your life?)

Job 3:20-25

Psalm 33:4

Psalm 51:17

Psalm 71:19-21

Proverbs 4:23

Matthew 7:9-11

Ephesians 4:31

Hebrews 12:15

James 1:2-4,17

Burden Bearers

Please be patient with me as I pass through the ugly stage of bitterness. It can be a long process, so try not to be judgmental. Pray that I will handle my anger in a God-honoring manner and that the Lord will guard my heart against invasive acidity of soul.

If you feel that I have been wallowing in self-pity for too long, prayerfully consider what (if anything) God might be asking you to share with me in an effort to help me see the destructive path I have chosen. But before any confrontation, be sure your own motives are pure, taking Matthew 7:1-5 and Luke 6:37-45 to heart.

anything for a child?

And she made a vow, saying, "O Lord Almighty, if you will
only look upon your servant's misery and remember me, and
not forget your servant but give her a son, then I will give him
to the Lord for all the days of his life, and no razor will ever be
used on his head."

1 Samuel 1:11

My flesh and my heart may fail,
but God is the strength of my heart
and my portion forever.

Psalm 73:26

*'King of Kings, who am I that I should even dare to approach your
throne? But I'm beyond desperate. Great Physician, I need your healing
hand upon both my defective body and my splintered heart. I would
give* anything *to hear the name "Mommy" called to my ears. I'll be a
godly mother and see that this child puts You first in everything.'*

*Almost before she realized what she was saying, she had committed
her future child to the life of a Nazirite (see Numbers 6). What had she
done, letting her emotions carry her to such a vow? This burden was
voluntarily taken by only a few, and typically for just a short season,
not for life.*

But there was no going back now. If the Lord's grace ever brought her the joy of labor pains, her son would live set apart, much like Samson, who had delivered her people from the Philistines after God placed him in the womb of his sterile mother (see Judges 13).

"I wish my family and friends understood my desire to be a mom," says Tina. "They say it's 'just natural.' To me, it's not just natural. It feels like I need to be a mom, like this is the one thing I'm meant to be."

For some, the inability to conceive is simply a closed door, and they have peace to move on to other life goals. For the rest of us, when children don't come along as planned, we face emotionally taxing, financially draining, and ethically complex choices. "Lord, I'll do *anything* for a baby!" can be the soul's gripping cry. But the moral and spiritual questions quickly arise: Is *anything* really okay?

For years we prayerfully and carefully considered what we could or should attempt in efforts to add children to our family: Is medical aid acceptable? If so, how far is too far? Do ends always justify means? What longing would (and would not) adoption resolve for us? Can I bargain with God or manipulate my way to motherhood? If my friends and family are pushing me toward treatment or adoption and we don't feel God leading us there, is there anything wrong with not taking these paths?

The authoritative source to answers all these questions is the Word of God. But even though we're all reading the same Bible, Christians often reach significantly differing opinions about acceptable options. I believe this can be attributed, at least in part, to the Holy Spirit's unique leading in each family. "For the word of God is living and active. Sharper than any double-edged sword, it penetrates even to dividing soul and spirit, joints and marrow; it judges the thoughts and attitudes of the heart" (Hebrews 4:12).

While there are some "black-and-white" scriptural constants, I must remember that the convictions God lays on my heart in "gray" areas, may or may not be applicable to others. Just as I don't want you to judge the choices I make with a clear conscience before the Lord, I cannot fault you for the paths He chooses for you, even when I would not personally have peace in the same decisions.

It all goes back to each person's need to listen for that still, small voice whispering to our hearts, "This is the way, walk in it." Then we must *walk* where He directs, as He prompts. Not *run* in our own directions ahead of His will or stubbornly dig in our heels, refusing to move forward.

If any of you lacks wisdom, he should ask God, who
gives generously to all without finding fault, and it
will be given to him.

JAMES 1:5

At the beginning of our journey, Rick and I looked for solid parameters through which to filter our goals and desires. With such guidelines we could easily redirect our course of action according to changing circumstances, but the moral plumb line against which we measured every choice remained constant.

Our friends John and Julie Donahue took this concept a step further. At the very early stages of investigating their options, they listed on paper exactly what they would and would not be willing to attempt in pursuit of children, looking long-range toward worse-case scenarios. They were very specific with things like "insemination only with husband's unwashed sperm." Then they took this commitment to another couple and asked for accountability.

For the most part they never wavered from these guidelines. On the rare occasions they felt a need to adjust their parameters, they could not rush into changes without prayerful evaluation because they knew they would need to provide their accountability partners with justification for such amendments. For example, when they understood the medical reality that inseminating with "unwashed" sperm would be a health hazard to Julie, they revisited their reasoning for this specific limitation.

Questions to Consider

With options ranging from intentionally *not* seeking family growth by any means other than the Lord's opening of the womb, to pursuing medical intervention, foster care, adoption, or other unique avenues, following are a few questions that may help you evaluate your choices. I exhort you to prayerfully consider your limitations *before* they become emotional realities. This way, when important choices must be navigated, you will know God's leading, not your heart's deception.

With each evaluation question I also share examples of ways God personally led and convicted Rick and me. I am not attempting to offer a comprehensive look at every path available to you. (A detailed, Christ-centered look at option specifics can be found in *The Infertility Companion* by Sandra Glahn and William Cutrer M.D.) Neither do I want to dictate your decisions, but rather to challenge you to consider God's leading for your family by illustrating some ways these parameters were applied in ours.

Are we "thoroughly equipped" to make choices in line with scriptural principles (2 Timothy 3:17)?

Do we know the Bible well enough to know how options are addressed? If not, it is time to get into the Word and find out. If we have already studied but can't find our issues directly addressed, what principles can we apply as we ask the Lord to give us wisdom and direction?

Sometimes we listen for His voice by searching Scripture, praying, and seeking the input of godly counselors, yet still find ourselves unsure about God's leading. When He seems silent, we can draw on what we know to be true from His Word, then simply make the best choices we can, asking God to confirm His plans for us by clearly opening and closing doors as we proceed.

Am I treating my body in a God-honoring manner?

If my body belongs to God, I must prayerfully consider the consequences of all that I do to and with this vessel. I wish I had more clearly educated myself about God's design for my body's reproductive abilities early in our journey. Understanding how and why mine wasn't properly functioning would have helped greatly in some of our decision making. (The book *Taking Charge of Your Fertility* by Toni Weschler, though not presented from a Christian worldview, is an excellent resource, explaining complex biological functions in understandable terms.)

Just as there is no sin in receiving medical aid for life-altering conditions like hearing loss or poor vision, there is nothing wrong with doctor involvement in helping my reproductive organs function according to God's intended design. The key to seeking medical aid is staying within God-honoring parameters. While medical assistance, in and of itself, is not ungodly, the Lord may call you personally to "be still," making intentional decisions not to pursue reproductive technology.

Do you not know that your body is the temple of the Holy Spirit, who is in you, whom you have received from God? You are not your own; you were bought at a price; therefore honor God with your body.

1 CORINTHIANS 6:19

Am I honoring God's view of children and upholding the sanctity of life?

Each option we consider must fully recognize our God-given obligations to value every child we create (including newly fertilized embryos) or for whom we take adoptive responsibility. There can be no question from Scripture that God holds a special love for children and views unborn babies as people with spirits capable of fellowship with Himself.

If you are unsure of when life begins, I plead with you to err on the side of caution, going back to the earliest *possibility* of the existence of a human soul when considering the need to protect the life of each child. When twenty-three chromosomes from each gamete (egg and sperm) align as a single cell, the DNA structure this child carries for the rest of his life is set in place. This amazing reaction offers me conclusive evidence that God has taken chemical components and created a new person.

Some state "life begins at conception," then attempt to redefine *conception* to be the time when a baby implants in the mother's uterus, thus negating all human life prior to implantation and invalidating the rights of fertilized embryos outside the body. But any biology class will confirm that conception is the beginning of a new entity of the same species as its parents. Place of conception (in or out of the mother's body) does not change the personhood of the conceived child.

Rick and I carefully considered IVF (in vitro fertilization — please see appendix C for explanation of this and other medical terms in this chapter). We decided we would not intentionally create more embryos in any given cycle than our doctor believed I could safely carry in a single pregnancy. Prior to treatment, we would establish provisions for the well-being of any embryos in the event either of us should be injured or die prior to transfer, stipulating that none of our babies could be abandoned, destroyed, or used for scientific research.

We would intentionally strive to avoid freezing embryos. Though many are able to justify the less-than-100-percent thaw ratio as being equivalent to natural miscarriage, we were uncomfortable with such statistics. We would resort to cryo-preservation if, for some reason outside our expectations, there were more embryos than anticipated or something happened in my cycle to prevent transfer that month.

We used these same principles when it came to IUI (intrauterine insemination). After an in-depth talk with our doctor, he agreed to perform a follicle reduction, aspirating from my ovaries and destroying (without allowing exposure to sperm) any additional eggs over the maximum threshold of babies he believed we could safely carry.

Sadly, some doctors take an aggressive approach to helping couples achieve pregnancy, then cope with the problem of "too many" babies by abandoning or destroying "extra" embryos or pressuring their patients into "selective reduction." In other words, many families are scared into aborting one of more of their babies in a multiple-gestation pregnancy, out of fear for the health of the mother or remaining children.

While I cannot support "health" abortions (such as the vast majority of selective reductions), when a mother's life is truly at stake and there is absolutely no hope for the baby, I believe God honors a choice to save one life, even at the cost of the other. Most ectopic and some rare uterine pregnancies would be valid examples. In about half of all ectopic pregnancies, the baby has already died before the process of removing her even begins.

If you have been forced to save your own life at the cost of your beloved baby, my heart grieves with you deeply. Have you ever considered that in order to save your life *eternally,* God gave the order for His Son to die too? He truly understands your heartbreak. May you know His peace that passes all understanding (see Philippians 4:7).

(For scriptural guidance about the beginning of life, see Psalm 22:9-10; 71:5-6; 139:13-16; Jeremiah 1:5; Matthew 10:42; 18:2-6,10-14; and Luke 1, paying special attention to the spiritual interaction of John and Jesus while both were still in the womb — for Jesus, just days after conception.)

Will this course of action hurt my testimony or become a stumbling block to others?

Rick and I wanted to make sure our lives would be a living testimony for God through our decisions. There are certain courses of action that we never considered because of their moral unacceptability.

Due to insurance changes, moves, and occasionally my choice to discontinue relationships with doctors I felt incompatible with, I worked with more than a dozen doctors through ten years of off-and-on treatment. I got to the point where I would begin an interview with a new doctor by stating up front, "Selective reduction is not an option."

Such a declaration set the stage for me to evaluate my doctor's views while allowing him to gain an appreciation for my convictions. If we got off on the wrong foot with this statement, I knew he wasn't a doctor I would be comfortable using to help me strive for motherhood. As difficult as it can be to find a doctor competent in the area of reproductive medicine, I've come to believe that whenever possible, my doctors should share my views, or at the very least go out of their way to respect them.

Are we honoring our marriage vows and God's desire for a mutually submissive, loving partnership?

"Marriage should be honored by all, and the marriage bed kept pure" (Hebrews 13:4). If either of us feels a betrayal of our commitment to one another on any level, this is not a direction we should pursue.

After one test revealed no living sperm in my body less than an hour after intercourse, we were advised that IUI was our only hope for conception. I was ready to proceed, but Rick was very uncomfortable with moving conception from the bedroom to the clinic. It wasn't even a moral issue, but simply one of preference. We prayed through all aspects of the decision (finances/stewardship, peace for God's timing, marital unity) and came to the conclusion that IUI was not the Lord's will for us at that time. I may never know the reason we couldn't go the IUI route at that time, but I know that God honors our decision to put our marriage vows above our own individual desires.

Are we using good stewardship?

God already owns all my money, time, abilities, and resources. What I have is a gift from Him. Is my pursuit of a child honoring His blessings, or squandering what I have been given? Am I investing more time and effort into the pursuit of parenthood than into my relationship with God?

I am called to trust God to fully provide the resources for whatever path He leads me to follow. Am I being faithful in my financial obligations to God (tithes and offerings) and others (debt)? Am I envious of those who seem to have more resources and abilities to grow their families? (Financial issues of fertility challenges give new meaning to "We can't afford to have kids.")

When we began seeking adoption, we were intimidated by the high cost of agency fees. Independent adoption through an attorney seemed to be more feasible. While I do know of several successful independent adoptions, the chance for adoption loss seems to be significantly higher than adoption through a credible agency. Considering the many heartbreaking private adoption leads we followed without ever bringing a baby home, I now see agency adoption as a worthwhile expense.

After wasting two years with a doctor who was not treating my condition properly (though I didn't know it at the time), I learned that just because a doctor lists "infertility" on his business card does not make him a specialist in the field. I wish I had known earlier to seek a referral to an RE (reproductive endocrinologist) when I hadn't conceived within the first year under the care of a gynecologist. While more expensive, I believe it would have been a wise use of our resources and would probably have saved both time and money in the long run.

Am I waiting on God's perfect timing?

I've often been able to relate to the woman who touched Jesus' cloak. She "suffered a great deal under the care of many doctors and had spent all she had, yet instead of getting better she grew worse" (Mark 5:26). During long periods when finances prevented steps toward adoption and our insurance wouldn't touch fertility treatment, I hated that feeling of "doing nothing." While friends were "actively" pursuing a baby, God wanted us actively waiting on Him. While God is the same "yesterday and today and forever" (Hebrews 13:8), He leads us to different options at different stages of our journey.

Many years into our pursuit of infertility treatment, my doctor prescribed thousands of dollars worth of medications that we were not financially in a position to purchase. It felt like a dead end. But in a matter of months, the Lord brought about a very unexpected change in jobs with better income and some infertility coverage. God gave Rick peace about proceeding with IUI, then literally sent a couple to our doorstep with a box full of fertility medication. As we waited on Him, the specific egg and sperm "recipe" needed to form our unique son was perfectly timed for the child God had ordained for our lives since before the foundations of the world.

Wait for the LORD;
be strong and take heart
and wait for the LORD.

PSALM 27:14

If this path ultimately leads to parenthood, can I explain to my child, without shame or secrecy, exactly how she joined our family?

She will want to know. Am I prepared to honestly explain when she is old enough to ask? If I don't tell her the truth, someone else somewhere, sometime, somehow will. How will we answer her questions five, ten, twenty years down the road?

Before we even knew what our specific medical issues would turn out to be, God strongly convicted both of us that any child added to our family should be genetically related to the two of us together (my egg and Rick's sperm) or to neither of us (various forms of adoption). This decision was based on our understanding of God's commands to keep the marriage bed pure.

Third-party conception can take several different forms, but it typically involves bringing the egg or sperm of a donor into the mix. It would mean that while neither of us would be engaging in extramarital relationships, we would still be bringing another man or woman into our marriage for the purpose of creating "half" of the child we had always dreamed of creating together. While we did not have peace with looking to third-party conception, I have witnessed several strong Christian families who have moved forward with this option in good conscience, believing that without extramarital relationships being pursued, the genetic materials themselves were a minor issue.

Is it both acceptable and beneficial in God's sight?

As embryo donation was just beginning to emerge as a life-saving option for "extra" embryos who, for a variety of reasons, could not be given a chance at birth by their genetic families, a dear family offered us the chance at a priceless gift. Adopting frozen embryos was an incredible, life-affirming option that might allow us the simultaneous joys of both pregnancy and adoption, without compromising our convictions about marriage.

Acceptability was not a question in our minds, especially in light of the 400,000 babies now in "frozen orphanages" in the United States alone. However, believing it to be medically unlikely that I could ever carry a pregnancy to term, we feared that transferring these babies to my body could well be their death sentence. While it was a painful decision, the question of benefit led us to decline parenthood, praying that God would raise up another adoptive family more physically capable of bringing these children to live birth.

Everything is permissible for me—but not everything is beneficial.

1 CORINTHIANS 6:12

Am I trying to force God's hand?

Sometimes God gives us less than the best He desires for us because we beg Him to do so, just as He conceded to the demands of Israel (see 1 Samuel

8:6-22). Am I trying to manipulate my way to a baby? Am I trying to bargain with God? Am I willing to accept God's best for my life, or do I want to be in the driver's seat and demand what I perceive to be best?

One of our adoption losses was especially painful. I had invested my heart in the life of a young birth mother and watched in awe as "our son" performed on the stage of his first ultrasound. I fell head-over-heels in love, only to be asked to support this woman as she chose a different family.

I asked, "Lord, how could you ask such a thing of me? Might a few well-spoken words swing the pendulum of parenthood back in our favor?" He answered clearly through the pages of His Word that morning in the hospital. Genesis 16 reminded me that while Sarah's plan *did* bring about the birth of Ishmael, everyone suffered as a result of her manipulation. I was strongly convicted that, as much as I craved this child, I had to let go.

For Further Thought

(Contributed by Denise England)

The Lord gifts people in many different ways. He has chosen to give us the gift of infertility. It is a gift that neither of us wanted. We spent over two years trying to deny, refuse, refund, or exchange this gift before finally, and with many tears, accepting it. God only gives good gifts, and I am continually learning that He chose to make us infertile because He loves us. He has bigger dreams for us than we even have for ourselves.

We invested more than two years and several thousand dollars into trying to conceive, but the Lord repeatedly confirmed that our gift would not be pregnancy, even though the reasons for our infertility are entirely unexplained. Through one heartbreaking disappointment after another, surgery, tests, and procedures, the Lord was humbling us and drawing us closer to Him. How many times did I crawl into my heavenly Father's lap and cry, pouring my heart out to Him like Hannah, begging for my blessing?

After two and a half years of trying, the Lord performed a miracle. He changed my heart and opened my eyes to the miracle of adoption, to my husband's delight. We are now in the process of adopting two precious children from Russia: a son, whom we will name William, who is sixteen months old, and a baby daughter, whose referral we are still awaiting. Although I will not have given birth to these children, my heart already knows that they are ours.

Infertility has left indelible marks on who we are as individuals and as a couple, but we are stronger, better, more in love with the Lord and with each other than we were before. Infertility is not an easy gift to bear, but we are learning day by day to thank the Lord for it.

Heart Treasures

Numbers 30

Psalm 119 (especially verse 133)

Proverbs 20:24

Jeremiah 10:23

Ecclesiastes 5:1-7

Matthew 7:1-5

Matthew 25:31-45

James 4:13-15

Romans 12:2

Romans 14:1–15:6

Jeremiah 17:9

Burden Bearers

Fertility issues are very personal. If I choose to share with you, I am placing a deep level of trust in our friendship. Before passing my news along to anyone else, please ask my permission.

Most fertility-related issues are medical problems, often entailing many complex issues. Infertility causes stress, but it is extremely rare for stress to be the sole cause of infertility. "Relaxing" will *not* cure endometriosis, open blocked fallopian tubes, enable deformed sperm to fertilize an egg, compensate for hormonal imbalances linked to recurrent miscarriage, or change my odds of carrying a child with genetic defects.

Don't suggest that my infertility will be resolved if I "just adopt." Adoption may (or may not) be a part of God's plans for us, but both infertility and adoption are issues we need to work through one step at a time. A healthy period of grieving for the biological child we may never have may be needed before we are ready to even consider adoption. And while I'm sure you know someone who adopted then got pregnant, statistically, adoption does not increase my chances of future pregnancy.

Please do not offer advice unless I ask you for it. I have probably already heard about (and tried) boxer shorts, vacation, and sexual techniques to improve our chances of conception. You might make very different choices in our situation, but as you are not in our situation, please keep your opinions to yourself unless you think we are acting in explicit contradiction to clear-cut biblical principles.

prayer, faith, and compassion

As she kept on praying to the LORD, Eli observed her mouth.

1 SAMUEL 1:12

Because of the LORD's great love we are not consumed,

for his compassions never fail.

LAMENTATIONS 3:22

She had sacrificed both her heartache and her future to the Lord. But that tender flicker of hope still struggled for life. She fearfully wondered what more God might ask of her if she remained in prayer. Her forefather, Jacob, had wrestled with the Lord, had demanded a blessing, and he had indeed been blessed. But Jacob lived with a limp for the rest of his life, a physical reminder of the battle (see Genesis 32:22-31).

Was it worth the risk? Yes, Hannah would pursue the Lord's blessings, whatever the cost. Even if the mending left a scar, it was time to break free from the self-imposed quarantine that held her heart captive. As tears gradually subsided, her lips moved in concert with the petitions of her soul, though her voice remained reverently silent before her Lord.

From his seat by the doorpost, Eli scrutinized the crumpled figure with perplexity. Could there be any reasonable explanation for such exhibition in the tabernacle courts? What trouble did this woman bring upon the house of the Lord?

For a long time Hannah's story brought me more distress than comfort, more anger than peace. My heart ripped to read how she dedicated her son to the Lord, then I became enraged that God would actually hold her to this life-long promise by taking her son from her. Through the years, every part of this tale has become precious to my heart. But if I had to pick just one topic that is especially tender to me, it would likely be the unfailing compassion of God, even when my faith has floundered.

It was a major breakthrough for me to realize that God never demanded Samuel of Hannah, but rather she offered the child of her heart of her own free will. I was unprepared to act on such a revelation for a time, but this truth was a significant starting point in my journey toward peace.

Hannah's nation had come to accept a terribly distorted view of faith, worship, and God Himself. Through a series of judges (Samuel would be the final man to fill such a role), God continually strove to turn a confused people back to Himself. Yet they repeatedly fell deeper and deeper into sin and the practices of the world, including the abhorrent practice of ritual child sacrifice. Scripture records several shocking testimonies of these acts of idolatry, such as "On the very day they sacrificed their children to their idols, they entered my sanctuary and desecrated it. That is what they did in my house" (Ezekiel 23:39).

When headlines pop up with stories about babies abandoned in garbage cans, I become livid. How could God allow such things? Imagine Hannah's anguish as a barren woman in a culture where children were burned alive in the name of worship. That she would keep on praying under these circumstances speaks greatly of her faith. In some ways, our situation today is similar, as we see children neglected and abandoned all around us. It can make us question God's plans and sometimes make it difficult to keep our faith strong.

During the first few years of our infertility journey, I was often challenged to have "more faith" so that God would expand our family. Like Job's comforters, friends fed me their insights on God's ways, often quoting bits and pieces of Scripture to support their claims. They focused intently on my need to be aggressive in asking of God, without leaving much room for His sovereignty in answering. What was intended as exhortation actually served as a stumbling block, feeding my notion that I should attempt to manipulate my way into motherhood.

A mother of three once wrote me a spiteful e-mail explaining God's great wisdom in preventing me from motherhood. She praised God that He had taken Noel from me without allowing her to be born and prayed that no birth mother would ever trust me with a child through adoption. She concluded that motherhood was a right earned only by godly women and that I was obviously receiving just judgment from God for something or I would not be experiencing a barren womb.

Did either my friends or my enemies have just cause to say that our fertility struggles were God's punishment for my lack of faith? Was I not "praying hard enough" or in the right manner? I felt like Hannah under Eli's scrutiny. I wanted my prayers to be acceptable to the Lord, yet it seemed others were constantly questioning my motives.

If *my* motives were right, then maybe I should lay the blame at my husband's feet? Maybe *he* didn't have enough faith. But then, how could I explain the conception of John the Baptist? Zechariah clearly questioned and doubted, yet his lack of faith didn't prevent God from allowing Elizabeth to conceive (see Luke 1:5-25). Likewise, Sarah's laughter didn't discredit the Lord's response to Abraham's faith (see Genesis 18 and 21). No, it didn't seem scriptural to blame my husband for this pain.

People said we needed *more* faith, so how much faith did we need to satisfy God's requirements for the healing of my reproductive organs? Jesus said faith as small as mustard seed (very tiny!) is enough to move a mountain. Mark 6:5 records that because of their lack of faith, Jesus could not do any miracle in his hometown "except lay his hands on a few sick people and heal them." In fact, Luke 17:11-19 records the healing of ten men, but only one is said to have had faith for his healing.

The more I study, the more I am convinced that when God wills, He moves, even when my faith is shaky. If I offer to Him the faith I have with the attitude of "I do believe; help me overcome my unbelief" (Mark 9:24), He does the rest. I am especially encouraged by the words of Jesus to Peter as He predicted Peter's betrayal: "But I have prayed for you, Simon, that your faith may not fail. And when you have turned back, strengthen your brothers" (Luke 22:32). In other words, "Your faith *will* falter, but then turn back to Me and let Me use this pain for good."

Faith Amidst Unanswered Prayers

I was born with a defect of my uterus causing conception difficulties as well as contributing to recurrent miscarriage. When I was being knit together in my own mother's womb, did God drop a stitch? How could I consider my broken reproductive organs to be wonderfully made? Jesus' interaction with a man born blind is enlightening:

> His disciples asked him, "Rabbi, who sinned, this man or his parents, that he was born blind?"
>
> "Neither this man nor his parents sinned," said Jesus, "but this happened so that the work of God might be displayed in his life." (John 9:2-3)

While it was a struggle to come to grips with God's hand in my suffering, there was also great freedom in realizing that my faith wasn't invalidated when prayers seemed to go unanswered. Of the many names listed in the Hebrews "Hall of Faith," Scripture states, "These were all commended for their faith, yet none of them received what had been promised. God had planned something better for us so that only together with us would they be made perfect" (Hebrews 11:39-40).

The apostle Paul pleaded repeatedly with the Lord to remove his "thorn in the flesh." Rather than relief from pain, God's answer was "My grace is sufficient for you, for my power is made perfect in weakness" (2 Corinthians 12:9). Jesus asked of His Father that He not be called to face the cross "if it is possible" (Matthew 26:39). Was it *impossible* for God to prevent the crucifixion? No! He is God and can do whatever He pleases. Was it imperative that God allow it for my sake, even when it was possible for Him to prevent it? Yes!

So Jesus, through perfect prayer with holy motives, through a direct audience with the Father, asked for God to do the possible, yet even Christ did not receive what He asked. His burden was not removed. His painful trial and execution were yet to be endured. If all is possible with God, yet He chose to say no even to the request of His beloved Son, can I not rest assured that trials that seem unbearable in my life fit much better in His perfect plan than anything I can imagine from my limited viewpoint?

We are twice told that God closed Hannah's womb. While we can look with the clarity of hindsight and see that He was preparing Hannah's heart so that her cherished son would be raised in a temple and bring a nation back to Himself, Hannah knew none of this then. In the same way, when I was in the middle of my deepest infertility heartache, I could not see how God was refining me and preparing my heart to better serve Him — both as a mother and through ministry. I did not know that my seemingly unanswered prayers were, in fact, being answered in a way I couldn't see then. Had I known, perhaps it would have been easier to keep my faith strong. But then it wouldn't have really been "faith" — would it?

What Kind of Faith?

While I do not know how anyone can survive the crushing grief of fertility challenges without a relationship with Jesus Christ, in one sense I think these trials may actually have been harder as a believer than if I were living in the world. Of course I know I could not have endured without His strength, but trying to understand the interaction between faith and prayer often left me hurting and confused.

One day, as I wrestled with God over these questions, He comforted me with the realization that struggling through disappointment with Him is not a sign of doubt, but rather proof of my faith. Hebrews affirms that God-honoring faith is as simple as coming to Him believing simply that He exists (see Hebrews 11:1, 6). If I believe He exists, it is reasonable that I might come to Him with preconceived notions of how He will answer. It is easy to trust when God's ways mesh perfectly with my plans. But it is only when reality collides with my preconceptions that my faith is tried and proved.

My friend Miriam shares,

> I am struggling very much with being angry with God. It is so hard not to feel disappointed. I feel like I have a right to have children, to not have my babies die. Why does God give to then take away? Why did I have to lose my babies before they were even born? What did I do wrong?
>
> Yet Something I can't understand is calming me down. Sometimes I am so mad I don't care to understand this soft, gentle Spirit. I was so close to God. I loved Him. I still do. I was totally impressed with Him and adored Him. I think that is why it is harder for me right now. I feel very much like a wounded lover. I am waiting for God to recapture my heart and to ignite my flame for Him again.

If I do not think there is a personal, caring, powerful God who is able to prevent or overcome my struggles, then I have no reason for disillusionment when He fails to meet my expectations. If I'm not expectantly waiting for those two lines to pop up on each home pregnancy test, what reason have I for tears with the start of each new period? If I don't believe God is capable of healing my body or saving my child's life, why bother with prayer when delivered disheartening news?

While I did frequently pray for healing, beg for conception, and plead for the lives of each of my unborn from the moment I knew they existed, I found that *demanding* prayers often left me short on peace. If I had "enough" faith, yet God still wasn't answering my prayers, what piece of the puzzle was yet missing? If it wasn't a matter of faith volume, then what kind of faith should I be pursuing?

Scripture's definition of faith leads to an interesting question: In what or whom am I placing my faith? Am I truly seeking after God Himself and His best plan for my life, or am I hanging my hopes on what I desire to see God do for me?

I was trying to make faith work according to *my* will while God's design was so much less complicated. He asked me only to come, to believe that He existed, and to earnestly seek *Him*. Instead I got caught up in the "rules" of my faith. I was looking for results from my perspective, while He was calling me to walk humbly with Him. The kind of faith He asked for was simple faith.

I stood on the need to "pray believing," thus trying to orchestrate every detail to God, explaining to Him how He must meet my custom orders. "Delight yourself in the LORD and he will give you the desires of your heart" (Psalm 37:4) was especially problematic for me. *If I do it your way, God, then You are obligated to reciprocate on my terms.*

It took me a long time to realize that I was treating the Lord as a give-to-get scheme. Jesus' name spoken over a prayer was never intended as a tool to bind God's hand to act according to my plans, but rather is another way of saying, "Thy will be done." To truly delight in the Lord was that missing puzzle piece. In my tunnel vision, I had overlooked the critical point of the entire verse.

To be clear on this point, please know I am not saying "just give up" on your prayer life. On the contrary, I want to exhort you to "keep on praying" like Hannah. But I know from firsthand experience how challenging prayer becomes when the same requests are continually lifted before the Throne and no tangible results are realized.

While it may seem futile, God wants me to bring my desires to Him. In fact James states simply, "You do not have, because you do not ask God" (4:2), so if I want God to act on my behalf, I should ask for my heart's desires. Like Jabez, the man whose name springs up in the dry genealogies of 1 Chronicles 4, I am encouraged to ask for blessings in abundance.

Bruce Wilkinson's little book *The Prayer of Jabez* was eye-opening for me on this issue. To be honest, I resisted reading it for a long time, fearing it would be more of the name-it-and-claim-it philosophy that had so shaken my faith before. But I was pleasantly surprised to find insights like this one: "The Jabez blessing focuses like a laser on our wanting for ourselves nothing more and nothing less than what God wants for us."[1]

If I really want results from my prayers, *how* should I pray? The Lord's Prayer offers a great model (see Luke 11:1-4). I must remember my place (God's holiness in heaven compared to my sinful state) and look to Him to fully meet my needs (daily bread). As Mark 11:24-25 confirms, to expect to receive anything I ask for, I must forgive others and ask for forgiveness of my sins as well. Temptation can not only be withstood, but also prevented when I ask God to keep me free from such entanglements (see Jabez's prayer in 1 Chronicles 4:10).

According to James 4:3, I also must be aware of my motives. Am I asking for selfish gain or for God's glory? As Jesus did, through trembling lips in the garden of Gethsemane, I must pray for God's will to be done above my own. That part, though it should be the easiest if I honestly believe in a loving God, is often the hardest step of all. C. S. Lewis is widely credited as having said, "We are not necessarily doubting that God will do the best for us. We are wondering how painful the best will turn out to be."

It can be a fearful thing to let go of my demands in exchange for God's plan. But when I do surrender to Him, seeking the best He has in store for my life, I am always amazed to find that I no longer feel I am settling for second best, because I have freed Him to act and freed my heart to accept His perfect plan. Wilkinson writes that the "radical aspect of Jabez's request for blessing [was that] he left it entirely up to God to decide what the blessings would be and where, when, and how Jabez would receive them." He goes on to describe such prayer as "radical trust in God's good intentions toward us."[2]

"Which of you, if his son asks for bread, will give him a stone? Or if he asks for a fish, will give him a snake? If you, then, though you are evil, know how to give good gifts to your children, how much more will your Father in heaven give good gifts to those who ask him!"

MATTHEW 7:9-11

For Further Thought

The rumors circulated about how Anna had been barren for the seven years her husband lived (see Luke 2:22-38). Others speculated about children that she might have buried along-side her beloved groom. Whatever her true story, they all shook their heads at the shame of her lonely state, without any living male relative to care for her in her advanced years.

Anna commented little on the gossip of the crowd, striving to live gracefully, not giving in to the anger and bitterness that could so easily have ruled her heart. Yes, a lifetime later, she still missed the man who was to have been her life-partner, provider, and protector. While her womb had dried up long ago, some days her arms still longed to be filled by the weight of an infant.

Like Hannah had nearly 1,000 years earlier, Anna took her heartache to the temple. As the years passed by, Anna devoted more and more of her time to prayer and fasting. The life she had envisioned for herself was replaced with a lifestyle of ongoing worship. Those who had once pitied Anna, now sought out the prophetess for her wisdom.

Over the past 400 years since He had last added to His written Word, it sometimes seemed as if God had forgotten His promise to redeem

Israel. But Anna's heart was stirred by strange things happening in recent months — Zechariah struck mute while performing his highest yearly duty, Elizabeth a mother in her old age, that young girl from Nazareth the center of scandal as she claimed to be a virgin, yet with child.

Simeon came frequently to the temple, so this day seemed to Anna like every other, until Simeon rushed to the young couple and took in his arms the infant they had brought for circumcision. At that moment Anna realized that all the heartache of her lifetime had been worth this one moment she now witnessed. Had it not been for her life taking so many seemingly "wrong" turns, she would not be in this right place at this perfect time. As the weight of this tiny One filled the ache of her arms, the last remnants of grief were erased from her heart as well. What joy that, as a direct result of years of grief and loneliness, she was now privileged to proclaim the Consolation of Israel!

 ## Heart Treasures

Job 42:2-3

Lamentations 3

Micah 6:6-8

Luke 17:5-6

Hebrews 11

James 1:2-8 (What specific gift does God promise to those who don't doubt?)

1 John 3:18-24

1 John 4:18

Burden Bearers

Wondering if God's perfect plan for my life will include children, or even realistically expressing painful doubts about my dwindling hope for the possibility of parenthood, does not equate to doubting God. Please don't judge my loss of hope about having a child to loss of hope in Christ.

You may say, "I just know God is going to give you a baby." But how do you know? Has He given you a revelation that He hasn't given me? Please be careful speaking for the Lord unless you are sure. (Prophets of old were stoned when they presumed to speak and their prophecies were found to be untrue.)

when churches add
to heartache

Hannah was praying in her heart, and her lips were moving but her voice was not heard. Eli thought she was drunk and said to her, "How long will you keep on getting drunk? Get rid of your wine."

1 SAMUEL 1:13-14

Let us then approach the throne of grace with confidence, so that we may receive mercy and find grace to help us in our time of need.

HEBREWS 4:16

Just as she seemed to be finding illusive peace, a stern voice of reprimand broke through her hallowed meditation. Hannah lifted her tear-stained face and locked eyes with the high priest. She sighed deeply, shoulders sagging. It had been a mistake to come. Her Tower of Refuge was just another place of misunderstanding and condemnation.

Was there anyone she hadn't offended today? First Elkanah complained because she wouldn't share in his meal. Now Eli had accused her of enjoying the bounty of the feast a bit too much. Crimson crept across her face as she thought of the intoxicated women rumored to frequent the entrance of the temple, not for worship, but to lead men into their bedrooms. What must Eli think of her?

She fought the temptation to flee, to draw back into isolation. But she had come too far to give up on the hope she was just starting to taste. Her vulnerable eyes implored the man to understand her need for grace.

When no one else seemed to comprehend our struggles, Rick and I turned to our church, believing we would find "mercy and grace to help us in our time of need" (Hebrews 4:16). Instead, as Hannah must have been, we were disillusioned. We looked to our pastor for moral guidance and watched him squirm under our blunt questions about medical options and reproductive ethics. We sought godly guidelines from which to measure our decisions and were instead advised to "just adopt." I begged the body of Christ to offer me biblically grounded answers about my baby's eternal security after death, only to find a double standard among many pro-life Christians who insist that a baby should never be aborted, yet treat a miscarriage as a nonperson.

Christians and critics alike have observed that the army of God often shoots its own wounded. Unfortunately, this remark holds true in the area of infertility support (or lack thereof). While many churches have wonderful programs for children, teenagers, singles, newlyweds, and families, their definition of *family* tends to only include those with children. When a childless couple is approached about ministry, the first invitation is often to work in the church nursery.

My purpose in this chapter is not simply to criticize the church. Instead I want you to know that if you're having trouble finding support within the Christian community, you are not alone. I'd like to offer some ideas and possible solutions to this widespread problem.

Like Hannah's, it seems the voices of the heartbroken often go unheard. When my dad represented Hannah's Prayer at a recent ministerial conference, he suggested that most churches had members of their congregations dealing with infertility or loss of children due to miscarriage or failed adoption.

Several pastors said, "Impossible! Not in my church. If it were so, I would know." The attitudes of a few of these leaders were heartbreaking. They were simply ignorant of one of the realities in their congregations.

Unfortunately, it's likely that there is at least one hurting family longing for a child, sitting in each church every Sunday. Even in a small church, statistically there are likely several families who have been touched by this very personal pain.

Think I'm being overly dramatic? My mail is filled with letter after letter from strong Christian families pouring out their anguish and frustration. Lack of church support in the midst of infertility, during adoption struggles, or after the death of a baby is a common theme. For those who are not strong in their faith to start with, the insensitivity of the Christian community often pushes them away from church altogether.

Dating clear back to Hannah and Eli, clergy members have a reputation (fairly earned or not) for being unsupportive of families in the midst of fertility challenges. While this is difficult to deal with, I'd like to suggest that most pastors and ministry leaders are not insensitive or uncaring. They are simply unaware of the struggles, the heartache, and the significant pain caused by infertility. (It's not something they usually talk about in seminary!) If you have been hurt by the seeming lack of concern on the part of a pastor, this is a time for mercy and grace to abound. Your pastor is human and may only need to be educated in order to be helpful to those with infertility issues.

What's So Hard About Church?

Beth writes,

> Baby dedications are so hard! At my church they are announced in advance, and I usually avoid them. I haven't attended a Mother's Day service in several years. The last one I attended was a nightmare. Not only was I sobbing uncontrollably and embarrassing myself, but I know that I put a damper on the

day for all those who were celebrating their children and being mothers. It took me weeks to get over it, especially the embarrassment of all the church members' questions and pity-looks at other services after the fact. For me, anything baby- or Mommy-related is now out. That's a tough thing at church since family and raising children is such a *huge* focus.

If these struggles are hard for church members, imagine ministering to an entire body of people when you, as a pastor, are the one facing such challenges. Clergy spouses often share devastating stories with me, either about how their spouses seem to "be there" for every other member of the congregation, yet "check out" of their own family heartbreaks. Or how both husband and wife share anguish while trying to learn to live with grief in the fishbowl of their congregation's criticism.

The single adjective possibly most applicable to fertility challenges is *lonely*. Joanie describes the isolation: "Last year I was so bewildered to learn that both my husband and I have infertility problems. Suddenly, I felt like I no longer belonged to the human race. In my circle of friends and acquaintances I do not know anyone who is going through this. I cried out before the Lord in prayer, complaining that this journey is too hard and lonely."

Unless I choose it for the purpose of drawing closer to God, isolation is suffocating. Jane says,

> I know that everybody is different in what they see as support, but I do wish that some of the people with whom we have shared our infertility would acknowledge that pain is still there. Despite the fact that it is pretty obvious that I am not pregnant, no one acknowledges that this is still a problem unless we bring it up again. It makes me feel pretty invisible.

The drama of fertility challenges often painfully performs on the stage of church participation. Public worship, in and of itself, opens the floodgates of my emotions so that I react to *all* stimuli more intently. Music is designed to open my spirit to connect with the Lord, but in so doing, it can also peel the scab off my hurting soul. Prayer is a window from my heart to God's. The Word of God is a double-edged sword that can painfully pierce my heart in ways I may not be able to publicly handle when I'm already so fragile.

I have often sat through a service unable to sing as the tears poured down my cheeks. Sometimes the source of tears is anger, sometimes feelings of abandonment and helplessness, sometimes longing and heartache, sometimes crying out to the Lord for the desires of my heart, sometimes asking why. And yes, sometimes in thankfulness for all the blessings in my life that I am so quick to overlook in the face of the baby struggles. These feeling are fine between God and me, but in church they easily become a public spectacle.

"Going to church is very difficult for me," says Janelle, four months after a full-term stillbirth.

> We had Samuel's funeral there and it's just too close to home. My pastor's wife said the reason people don't approach me is because I look like I'm about to cry when I'm there. I told her that I am about to cry. It's rare for me not to shed a tear or two during church.
>
> Our very small congregation includes five babies right now, all noisy, so it's hard for me not to notice them during the service. I do think it will get "easier," although I hate to even say that. How can grief over a lost child ever be easy? I think time makes the pain less sharp; how much time, I don't know. I still have many days where I break down at home.

After attending church on our second Mother's Day of infertility, I became despondent. I tried to read my Bible and pray, but my prayers came out as angry shouts at the Father I felt had abandoned me. It was out of that week that God taught me some incredible lessons that have eased me through the subsequent years of infertility, failed adoptions, and miscarriages. However, I think one of the most important lessons I learned is that there are times when attending church is more harmful than helpful.

When Church Isn't the Answer

When intentional, loneliness can actually be healing: "Jesus often withdrew to lonely places and prayed" (Luke 5:16). I realize the following may be controversial advice, but I believe withdrawal is sometimes necessary. If you struggle with this section, put it in the category of, "I, not the Lord," as the apostle Paul wrote of some of his own insights.

Several years ago, Rick and I were attending a church that had many problems, ultimately resulting in a church split. About the same time, we moved half an hour away. We said we would find a church home in our new community and start fresh. While we did sporadically look for a new body, our hearts were not in the search. It was six months before we really tried to plug into a new congregation.

That half-year was a lonely, dry time in our lives. But from the infertility perspective, the break from corporate worship was the best thing we could have done. By stepping away from the weekly exercise of church attendance, we were able to experience a needed hunger for fellowship again. Finding a good church family became something we deeply longed for, understanding how important it was to "not give up meeting together, as some are in the habit of doing" (Hebrews 10:25). Church became a joy and privilege again rather than just a tiresome routine.

The break helped me gain a better perspective that worship is about God, not about me. I learned that even as Hannah cried out to God in anguish in the temple, I could cry in church without shame. But if I had permission to cry, I also must wholeheartedly enter into praise and worship just as Hannah did (even *before* God granted her heart's desire; see 1 Samuel 1:19).

So, here's the part that's bound to raise eyebrows. When I find couples who are deeply struggling with church attendance, I often suggest that they pray about taking a break for a while. I suggest this because I know how helpful it was for us to be away from church for a short time. If your heart leaps with hope at this suggestion, please heed these strong warnings and safeguards:

Pray. Before you make a choice to stop attending church, even for a few weeks, pray, Pray, PRAY about this decision. Do you need a break to be refreshed and hungry for worship again, or is this a time God is calling you to offer the "motions" of church attendance to Him as sacrifice, trusting Him to bring your heart in line in His timing? If you don't have peace that God is leading you to take a vacation from attendance, don't do it.

Set a return date. If, after careful prayer, you feel that God has freed you to step away from church for a while, set a specific period of time. At the same time you make the decision to take a break, mark a date on your calendar when you will be back in church, then stick to it. Much less than four weeks and there may be little benefit. Letting more than twelve weeks pass makes it very hard to go back, but as He did with us, God may call you to take a break for longer.

Contact your pastor. Before you take the break, you may want to talk with your pastor, or at least write him a note. Explaining your situation may help him be more sensitive with other families as well. If you aren't comfortable sharing details, ask for his prayers as you deal with family matters that will require you to be away from church for a time.

Honor commitments. Your commitments should still be honored. Do you have an obligation within the church, such as teaching Sunday school or serving on the worship team? Can you help find a substitute or replacement if you need to go before your commitment expires? And don't forget tithes and offerings!

Consider other ways to participate. Consider if you want to stay plugged into your church family, or if that would be defeating the point of your break. Are you involved in a small group or Bible study that you'd like to continue? In what alternate means of fellowship can you participate?

Evaluate your goals. Would a simple change of scenery serve the intended purpose? Perhaps your church has an evening or mid-week service that is less child-oriented. Maybe, rather than taking a set block or time away, taking specific pain-trigger days off, such as Mother's Day, might be beneficial.

Visit other churches. This may be a time to visit other churches. I'm not advocating "church hopping." Remember, there is a set time frame with the intention to return to your home body at the end of this short season.

Worship as a family. If God is calling you to a short season of total isolation, be sure to set aside regular time to pray, praise, worship, and study as a family. Jesus did not withdraw to a lonely place for the sake of being lonely, but for the purpose of prayer.

God Is Still There

When your church doesn't "get it," God is still there. Scripture says, "Jacob was left alone, and a man wrestled with him till daybreak" (Genesis 32:24). Use your alone time wisely to wrestle through some tough issues with the Lord. "The [grieving person] who is really in need and left all alone puts her hope in God and continues night and day to pray and to ask God for help" (1 Timothy 5:5). Put your hope in God!

Where did Jesus turn when even those who should have been most attuned to ministry contributed to His heartache? "During the days of Jesus' life on earth, he offered up prayers and petitions with loud cries and tears to the one who could save him from death, and he was heard because of his reverent submission" (Hebrews 5:7). His actions are a reminder to seek the Father when the isolation of grief becomes unbearable.

You are invited to come boldly to the throne. The Most Holy Place, once reserved only for a yearly visit from the high priest, was made accessible to you at the moment of Jesus' death, when "the curtain of the temple was torn in two from top to bottom" (Mark 15:38).

Scripture is clear that we may come directly to the Lord with our needs. Don't make the mistake of putting your pastor on a pedestal or feeling like you can only talk to God through your priest. If you aren't finding the mercy and grace you long for from your church, don't give up on God.

Hannah had nowhere to turn other than the tabernacle. But then "the Word became flesh and made his dwelling among us. We have seen his glory, the glory of the One and Only, who came from the Father, full of grace and truth" (John 1:14). That Jesus "made his dwelling" can literally be translated that He "tabernacled" among us. Again I find reason to thank the Lord that we are no longer under the Law that bound Hannah, but under grace that sets people free.

———————

"So if the Son sets you free, you will be free indeed."

JOHN 8:36

———————

For Further Thought

While Hannah knew the place to take her pain, Eli had good reason to worry about her. When God seems silent, it is all too easy to turn to other coping mechanisms. Are you struggling with alcohol, an eating disorder, sexual temptations, or any other source outside God's offered strength? God desires to set you free from these entanglements. Please revisit chapter 3, and lay your burden down.

Heart Treasures

Genesis 32:22-32

Psalm 77 (Verse 4 has an interesting parallel to Hannah's experience.)

Jeremiah 17:7

Matthew 23:23

Ephesians 3:12

Ephesians 5:18-20

Hebrews 10:19-25

1 Peter 3:8

Burden Bearer

Feel free to offer suggestions for areas of church involvement I might not have considered, but please don't take personal offense when I need to step away from activities or say no to ministry opportunities. These things may be possible for me in future seasons, but for now I may need time to heal and seek God's plan for my life, which is turning out so very different from what I had anticipated.

As I seek to find my place as an infertile woman in the body of Christ, it may take some adjustments for me to find where I feel best used of the Lord. For instance, the church nursery might be exactly where I *want* to be on some days when my arms just ache to hold a baby, but it might just as easily become a place that stabs my heart with envy and grief over what I do not have. Our woman's Bible study may feel more like a "moms' club," where I'm an outsider, than a place I can freely fellowship and nourish my soul on the Word of God.

anguish and grief

"Not so, my lord," Hannah replied, "I am a woman who is deeply troubled. I have not been drinking wine or beer; I was pouring out my soul to the LORD. Do not take your servant for a wicked woman; I have been praying here out of my great anguish and grief."

1 SAMUEL 1:15-16

This is what the LORD says:
"A voice is heard in Ramah, mourning and great weeping,
Rachel weeping for her children and refusing to be comforted,
because her children are no more."

JEREMIAH 31:15

Her heart petitioned the name too holy to voice, 'Yahweh, will I ever have a labor story to share with the women at the city well? How I long for morning sickness! Will I know the joy of snuggling my child to my breast? Could it truly be that I may never watch my own chubby-legged infant attempt his first tottering steps? Will Elkanah ever have the chance to direct our offspring in Your ways? Will I ever cry as I send my son off to his first day of studying the Torah? Might I never be mother of the bride?'

A lifetime of losses overwhelmed Hannah. As she grieved for the child who was not, Elkanah's attempts to comfort her were futile.

Distraught beyond words, absorbed in prayer, now she must muster a defense against Eli's misjudgment.

Society teaches us that reproduction is ours to control. Shock and sorrow accompany the discovery that we cannot always plan parenthood. Infertility is prolonged grief with few defined points of closure. Anguish is caused by the death of dreams, not always by the death of an individual.

Because there are few ways to memorialize the profound loss of a child who never existed, it can be an agonizingly extended grief without validation. Fresh waves of trauma are triggered by anything from watching the school bus picking up your neighbors, to a baby shower invitation in your mailbox, to the lasting legacy of not being able to brag about your grandchildren later in life. Just as Hannah pleaded with Eli, you pray people won't harshly judge you while your heart sits shattered at your feet.

Truly infertility or the loss of a child brings deep grief, but does God's Word validate such anguish? In addition to holding many accounts of barren characters carefully preserved for our benefit, the Bible treats childlessness as truly devastating pain. Proverbs 30:15-16 lists barrenness right up there in the "top three" things that never are satisfied, along with death, drought-devastated land, and fire. When prophesying Jesus' betrayal and crucifixion, Isaiah 53 talks of the Lord having no descendants, noted with as much seriousness as are the oppression and affliction that ultimately led to His murder.

While many people think of infertility only as failure to conceive, the medical definition also encompasses conceiving without giving live birth to a child. Ramah, the town where Hannah endured so much sorrow over her barrenness, held prophetic significance. As foretold by Jeremiah, many future mothers would weep there.

> When Herod realized that he had been outwitted by the Magi, he was furious, and he gave orders to kill all the boys in Bethlehem and its vicinity who were two years old and under,

in accordance with the time he had learned from the Magi. Then what was said through the prophet Jeremiah was fulfilled: "A voice is heard in Ramah, weeping and great mourning, Rachel weeping for her children and refusing to be comforted, because they are no more." (Matthew 2:16-18)

The History of My Grief

The first six to eighteen months of infertility were the hardest for me. These were the months I was still learning to process the reality of unfulfilled expectations, before God had broken me free from the worst of my bitterness. Not knowing if we could ever conceive, my daily grief in the *now* was always shadowed by fear of all the *tomorrows* without a baby.

We faced our first adoption-related loss at about the sixteen-month mark. So, added to the pain of not being able to bring these two children into our family was the sudden realization that adoption might not be such an easy answer to our dreams of parenthood.

Noel's conception and miscarriage marked a significant turning point in our journey. It was possible that I had had early miscarriages in the past, but this was our first *known* pregnancy. Noel's life brought hope because we now knew pregnancy was achievable, but it also added a new dimension to our heartache.

My first reactions were shock and denial. Beyond the initial tears, I was numb. I could not laugh, cry, or experience any kind of emotional reaction. I was going through the motions of daily life in a fog. For well over a year I had cried every month with my period anyway, so I tried to convince myself this had just been another late cycle.

It took me five months to acknowledge that I had indeed been pregnant and lost a baby. When I could finally face the reality of miscarriage, my emotions were like the breaking of a dam. I sobbed for hours, inconsolable, then spent the next several months on the fragile verge of tears over anything and everything. It was nearly a year before we told most of our family or friends about Noel's short life.

Sometimes my mind taunted me with the question "Was I really ever pregnant?" After much prayer I felt a need to name our baby. Because we didn't know her gender (though we both thought of her as a girl), we searched for unisex names that would have significant meaning to us. My short pregnancy had encompassed Christmas Day, thus Noel seemed fitting. We teamed this with the middle name of Alexis, meaning "minister of needs," because we felt she was a gift of encouragement from God, making us parents, even if only to a child in heaven.

Because Noel's death was distinct from any other single event in the previous two-year blur of infertility grief, she allowed me to focus my sorrow on a specific loss rather than only on an illusive dream, and in that fact I did find some consolation. Many couples initially enter the world of fertility challenges by way of loss, only then to face the inability to conceive again or to face more losses. There is no realistic way or useful reason to measure which journey is more painful, as either course is deeply anguishing.

In a strange way, Noel's short life brought healing to at least one set of scars that infertility had inflicted on my heart. I could acknowledge my heartache by wearing a special piece of jewelry in my baby's honor, by placing a memorial ornament on our Christmas tree, by telling anyone who would listen that I was a mother now. These were all things robbed from me by the intangible nature of nonconception.

For me, it truly was "better to have loved and lost then never to have loved at all," but oh so painful! While her very existence was therapeutic, I do not want to minimize the horror of Noel's death. Conception did not remove us from the infertility journey; it only moved us into a new leg of a painful course. Empty arms of barrenness became the empty arms of bereaved parents.

I dreaded the intended comfort, "At least now you know you can get pregnant." Prior conception was no guarantee that future pregnancy would be possible. Even if I could conceive again, I had no track record to assure myself that pregnancy could end in live birth. And should the Lord be gracious enough to allow us to bring home a living baby in the future, no child could replace this unique one I had just lost.

Each child lost is a significant reason for grief. Of her miscarriage, Raegan said,

> I would have loved to have gotten flowers from someone, since that is a common practice in our society when a loved one passes. My biggest problem throughout this entire ordeal has been gaining other people's acknowledgment that I was even pregnant with a real live baby. I just wanted someone other than my husband to acknowledge that our baby died.
>
> My best friend from college finally cornered me and asked pointblank how I was truly feeling. She listened, more than anyone had before that point. That's what I needed! She openly admitted that she couldn't understand what I am going through, but did say that she knew I had lost my baby. It helped so much just to have someone say it.

Some women are able to birth a house full of kids without a single death, while others face the trauma of recurrent losses. Ruth writes, "One thing that hurt was that although many people sent cards the first time I miscarried, only one or two did the second time. It made me feel like they thought, 'Oh well, you're used to it.'"

Joel Samuel and Hannah Rose were our second and third known miscarriages, our ninth and tenth losses when including the grief of our unsuccessful adoption attempts. A few weeks after Hannah's death, I came home to find a gourmet fruit basket sitting on my doorstep with a simple note of sincere sympathy. The friend who sent this gift realized that my children mattered and my grief was real. Their lives were being fully validated, just as if they had been born, lived outside the womb, and been buried. I will forever cherish the sweet taste of those beautiful pears.

One out of every 115 babies in the United States is stillborn. This is about twenty-five thousand children every year who are carried past twenty weeks of pregnancy (the generally accepted landmark that separates "miscarriage" from "stillbirth"), only to be born dead. The cause of stillbirth can be determined in less than half of all cases, adding to the questions, fears, and grief families must process.

While most women are able to give live birth to a subsequent child, about 3 percent of women who have suffered one stillbirth will know this anguish more than once. When Christie gave birth to Noah, her firstborn, no cries met her ears. A little more than four years later, after the joyful births of two daughters, Christie and Glen were again faced with the news, "I'm sorry; we cannot find a heartbeat," at twenty weeks.

In an effort to find *something* to say, people have tried to console Christie with such irrational statements as "Now you don't have to worry about the inconvenience of being up nights with a crying baby." Christie's reply is "I have sleepless nights anyway, only I'm the one crying." To those who strive to comfort with "At least you didn't get to know him," she grieves, "That's one of the most painful parts about this. I don't even have memories to cherish."

The week Simon should have been due, Christie reflected,

> It would be crazy and busy and exhausting. . . . I want that so much! I want labor and giving birth. I want breastfeeding and being up half the night. It was so hard to lose Noah, to have empty arms and an empty house. I felt so left out. I wondered if we would ever have children. Simon's death is hard in different ways. I know exactly what I am missing. I don't have time to grieve and I don't have the emotional energy to parent, so I do neither very well.

When Miriam lost Gioia to Turner Syndrome twenty-four weeks into her pregnancy, she realized that grieving is a learned skill.

> I did not go to church yesterday; I just couldn't face the crowd of people. A friend came later to see me and I cried as I tried to explain to her why I didn't want to go to church and why it hurt me so much. I know I have to grieve. . . . But I don't know how to grieve! No one ever taught me how! Actually, no one ever taught me that grief is okay for a Christian.
>
> I don't know how to show my feelings, because every time I have in the past shown the depth, people just feel so sorry and try to find ways to stop it. I think they confuse comforting with stopping the flow of tears.

A friend recently pointed out to me that when Lazarus died, Jesus, knowing He was only moments away from bringing His friend back to life, still wept. Yes, God swallowed up death in victory at the cross, but there is a legitimate time and need to express all the anguish you feel over the person missing in your life. Grief is a part of God's design for human emotions. Popular Bible study author Beth Moore writes, "God's Word never said we were not to grieve our losses. It says we are not to grieve as those who have no hope (1 Thess. 4:13). *Big difference.*"[1] As believers we always have hope in the One who created us in His image and has plans for us that we cannot even comprehend.

Christians sometimes have a funny idea about sorrow being unspiritual. We often expect grieving hearts to heal quickly, without allowing for the many stages of the grief process. Pam writes, "Our Savior was 'a man of sorrows and acquainted with grief' (Isaiah 53:3). I wonder if He came to one of our churches now like that, if someone wouldn't try and cheer Him up and tell Him to 'let it go and open himself to the joy of Lord,' then give Him a book and tape series to that effect?"

I am in deep distress. Let us fall into the hands of the LORD, for
his mercy is great; but do not let me fall into the hands of men.

2 SAMUEL 24:14

I often talk of "the loss of a child" through this book. This specific phrase is actually one of my *least* favorites because it seems to sugarcoat death. Stating that a family has "lost" their child can also sound accusatory or careless, as if they have simply misplaced something of little value. I use this phrase only because I haven't found a more concise way to encompass both the death of a child *and* failed adoption grief.

The Grief of Adoption Loss

Adoption loss is to the death of a child what divorce is to widowhood. They are circumstantially different griefs, each with significant unique challenges, but the ultimate outcome of each, being without your loved one, holds the same core anguish. An adoption lead that doesn't end in an addition to your family is similar to miscarriage. A child who comes home with you but doesn't stay is a grief much like that of stillbirth or infant death.

I am a huge advocate of adoption and have seen far more success stories than disappointments. But as there are so few resources for adoption failure, this book would not be complete without addressing the genuine grief that accompanies such losses. There are as many kinds of potential adoption losses as there are ways to adopt.

In her touching book *Things Pondered,* Beth Moore shares the joys and struggles of raising her son Michael for seven years, then relinquishing him back to his birth mother. "I have never before experienced this kind of stabbing pain and loss," she writes. "Words defy an explanation of the emotions my family has experienced."[2]

I've known families who were matched with birth families, only to be stunned when their children were stillborn. Another family's son died of malnutrition before the paperwork was finished for them to go bring him home from overseas. I've even heard a few heartbreaking stories in which children had such severe attachment disorders that adoptions had to be reversed for the safety of family members.

Foster-parenthood can be full of rich rewards, but sending children back home can be very hard. When you participate in a foster-to-adopt program, the emotional ups and downs of waiting to see what children will become permanent family members can leave you feeling like a yo-yo.

Rick and I entered marriage with the idea of growing a large family, built through both birth and adoption. When pregnancy didn't happen quickly, we spread the word that we wanted to adopt. Over the years, several potential leads came our way. Many times God made it clear from the start that a specific situation wasn't the one He had planned for us. But five times (including two sets of siblings) we let our hearts begin to hope and dream that just maybe these leads were intended to be our kids.

In our first adoption attempt, God painfully, yet peacefully, led us to say no as we understood more about the needs of a preschool-aged brother and sister we were longing to adopt. Twice we were "in the running" to adopt babies, but both birth moms ended up choosing the other family they were considering each time. *(Okay, God, what's wrong with us?)* Once the birth mom we were working with made a last-minute choice to raise her baby. And our last loss, the twins who had stolen our hearts through ultrasound pictures and hours and hours of conversation with their mother, in the end proved to be a heartbreaking adoption scam with a woman who was never even pregnant.

As hard as our fruitless adoption leads were, I count us blessed to have endured such relatively "easy" situations. Steve and Nancy lost not only their hearts, but also thousands of dollars to a woman who, while indeed pregnant, fraudulently misrepresented herself as *still* pregnant for an entire month after her baby's birth. As they awaited the adoption, Nancy was preparing her body to nurse, so when the deception became evident, she had to go through the hormonal changes of stopping lactation and the physical anguish of breast engorgement while trying to process the emotions of betrayal and loss.

While the birth mother was actively choosing to raise her daughter she was accepting financial and material support from my friends, claiming to intend to place her baby for adoption upon birth. She ended up in jail (on charges unrelated to adoption fraud), her newborn daughter in the foster system, and Steve and Nancy with empty arms until God led them to become foster parents. (They have since been blessed with a six-week-old boy they are now in the process of adopting.)

Probably the hardest part of adoption loss is not knowing how the lives of each of these children turned out. Each of the children we hoped to adopt had become "ours" in our hearts for a time. Yet we do not know where they are or how they are. This is difficult, but I believe I have an idea of God's reasoning for even these heartbreaks. He allowed these children to touch our lives, and He is now using us as personal prayer warriors in their lives (as well as in the lives of the biological families involved). I may never know, this side of heaven, God's plans for these precious ones, but I can pray for them always. What a blessing to be used in this way!

How amazing it will be to one day see what part my prayers played in God's plans for the children who share my heart, though not my home. In the midst of their losses, could either of Moses' mothers (biological or adoptive) ever have dreamt the plans God had in store as He fashioned and strengthened this man through many painful twists, turns, and separations in life?

Those sensationalized adoption loss stories that hit the evening news from time to time only happen to "somebody else." That's what I always thought anyway. Until the day my friend Jennifer called to say that after raising their son since birth, she and her husband, Brad, were now entrenched in a custody battle with Nathaniel's biological father, a two-time convicted felon, who had abandoned his girlfriend as soon as he learned of her pregnancy. Just weeks before Nate's first birthday, he was taken from the loving arms of the only parents he had ever known to live with a man he had only recently met through court-ordered visitations.

Three days after releasing Nate, Brad shared,

> We know it's far from over, but right now all we can do is focus on getting through today, and being there for our daughter, who continues to break down in tears when she thinks of her brother. Every night she prays that he is safe in his new home. Only those who have walked this road know how bad it hurts right now.
>
> Every day seems to be harder than the day before. And every day we think of him, what he's doing. Is he sleeping at night? Is he crying for Mom and Dad? Does he think we didn't want him anymore? Someone told me that this would be harder than a death, and now I understand. There's no closure, only questions.

A few days later Jennifer wrote,

> We're lost and empty inside. . . . Please continue to pray for us and for our precious Nathaniel. Our hearts are filled with worry and hurt at the thoughts of what he must be going through without Daddy and Mama. I have not been able to touch his things yet. I woke a few nights ago, thought I heard him crying. I will always wonder about him, as if he was kidnapped.
>
> We all can use the prayers still. We don't know how or where to go from this point. Tomorrow we will go to church, the first Sunday without Nathaniel and also Brad's birthday. It will be a hard and emotional day!

As of the writing of this book, Brad and Jennifer are working to change California law to require judges to look at the best interests of the child in any adoption custody hearing, as is already required of foster-care placements. (Ongoing updates about Nathaniel's Law and cases where other families face the potential of similar devastating losses can be found at www.babynate.org)

Mordecai had a cousin named Hadassah, whom he had brought up because she had neither father nor mother. This girl, who was also known as Esther, was lovely in form and features, and Mordecai had taken her as his own daughter when her father and mother died. When the king's order and edict had been proclaimed, many girls were brought to the citadel of Susa. . . . Esther also was taken to the king's palace and entrusted to Hegai, who had charge of the harem.

ESTHER 2:7-8

For Further Thought

(Contributed by Pamela Houghton)

In the Old Testament, a person in grief tore his robe and didn't run out to Kohl's to get a new one to go to church. Women cut their hair. Men shaved their beards. There was weeping and wailing. For a whole year, nobody expected you to look or be the way you were. How wonderful! But in our nutty society, the person who "keeps it together," who's "so brave," and who "looks so great — you'd never know," that's who is applauded.

Grief is not the opposite of faith. Mourning is not the opposite of hope. I believe that well-meaning Christians can try to hurry us out of our mourning because we make them uncomfortable. The Bible does not say to cheer up the bereaved, but rather to "mourn with those who mourn." Christ does not say we grieve because we are deficient in faith, but rather, "Blessed are those who mourn, for they will be comforted [not *rushed*]" (Matthew 5:4).

Heart Treasures

Exodus 2:1-15

Psalm 10:14

Psalm 31:9

Psalm 34:18

Psalm 42

1 Peter 1:6-7

Burden Bearers

(Adapted from a letter by Scott and Michele Pickle, a year after their IVF twins [after five years of infertility] were born sixteen weeks early. Grace lived two days. Gideon fought twice as long before he too went to be with the Lord.)

We need to talk about our children . . . sometimes. How we miss them, how we remember them, how unfair life was to them. How they had our toes, fingers, mouths. How wrong it is that a mother cradles her child while taking her off life support. How wrong it is that someone else held our son as he died.

Sometimes we need to talk about how we feel. How guilty we feel for things we could never foresee, or fix. How we wonder if we made bad choices, or misunderstood God's will for us. How unfair it is that so-and-so is pregnant *again*. How frustrating it is that we are treated delicately, like broken people. Or that we are spoken to insensitively, as if we should "be over it by now." How, when we walk in a room, we feel everyone thinks of us as "the couple who lost their children." How, when we walk in a room, no one knows or cares that we lost our children.

Sometimes we need to hear how you feel. We don't need you to fix us, to be all-knowing, all-understanding. We want to hear your feelings about our children, but should just as often incorporate thoughts about your own lives. It's comforting to hear about and participate in other people's pain.

Always remember to whom you speak. Yes, this conflicts with the above need. Consider this: Your sense of joy from the accomplishments of your baby is a sting, not a comfort; and yet we do want to know how you and your young ones are faring. Your elation of pregnancy is a reminder of our loss; and yet we do want to know about and be involved in your pregnancy. Invite us to showers, just don't be surprised if we politely decline. Your frustration toward caring for your children falls on the wrong ears with us; still we want to be there to help out. If we can do something constructive, we would love to, just don't use us to vent frustration. Our lives do not revolve around the care and welfare of our children, so when we drop out of a roundtable discussion on the topic or politely move on to something different, don't be surprised.

We need *not* to talk about our children . . . sometimes. This world, as cruel as it can be, is a place of wonder and excitement, meant for our enjoyment. We need to be reminded of that. We need to laugh and to make new memories. We cannot too often dwell on the past, not so as to erase it, but rather to augment our lives with a salting of the good in this world, those of great import or little consequence.

Above all, we still need time. We continue to hold onto hope and take active steps to bring additional children into our lives. The thoughts and process consume more than anyone knows. Yet we may or may not choose to discuss our pursuit. The pressure of achieving success is increased with each person we engage on the topic. We need more time to heal, to feel normal, to discover what God's plan for us is. Asking for time from friends and family may be a self-centered thing, but it's what we need. Don't take our quietude, seclusion, or self-centered set of expectations personally. We just need time.

ministering peace in the body of Christ

Eli answered, "Go in peace, and may the God of Israel grant you what you have asked of him."

1 SAMUEL 1:17

Keep watch over yourselves and all the flock of which the Holy Spirit has made you overseers. Be shepherds of the church of God, which he bought with his own blood.

ACTS 20:28

This face did not match his preconceived ideas of the woman who had been prostrate on the temple floor. Eli had expected hardness etched by a life of sin. Instead he was stunned by strange beauty, tainted with raw grief, yet softened by a radiant grace. What could cause these haunting eyes to look so troubled when her face could almost be described as glowing? The priest recalled descriptions of Moses' countenance after meeting with the Lord on Mount Sinai (see Exodus 34:29-35).

True worshipers were rare those days, but she surely was one. While questions swirled through his mind, Eli realized he didn't need to give or receive answers nearly as much as he needed to acknowledge her obvious anguish and share with her in committing this pain to the Lord. Her sincere faith demanded the touch of a great God. He prayed the Lord might use him to offer this woman a fresh start. What joy to minister peace to a hurting heart! **"**

In chapter 12 we discussed several complaints about churches' handling of fertility challenges. If I were to share grievances without offering solutions, there would be little use for this book. I can't offer a perfect fix, but I can supply a toolbox designed to help repair past hurts while proactively preventing much future damage. I have written this chapter with ministry leaders in mind. Perhaps you are a leader in your church and can help bring new awareness to other members of church staff. Even if you're not a ministry leader, this chapter will offer ideas of how to help those in your church minister more effectively to those struggling with infertility, miscarriage, or adoption loss. If you feel comfortable, this would be a chapter to pass along to your pastor or other church leaders. If not, you may want to find ways to talk with your pastor about some of the ideas here, opening up a respectful dialogue with the goal of helping leaders be more aware of struggles within their congregation.

In recently conducting an informal survey of about two thousand families facing a wide range of fertility challenges, I was somewhat surprised at their answers to my simple question, "What one thing has someone said or done that was most helpful or most hurtful?" The scenarios they described were not unusual, but personal reactions were vastly contradictory from one individual to the next. A situation cited as "most comforting" to one family could easily be viewed by another as a devastating experience.

When working with broken people, attempts to minister can easily inflict significant, though unintentional, pain. With the diversity of human emotions and experiences in mind, there is no cookie-cutter answer, no perfect ministry template that can be applied to every church or grieving family.

So, if this is a no-win situation, why even try? If people are going to get their feelings hurt no matter how earnestly a church attempts to bless them, what's the point? The key is an attitude of grace. While intent may sometimes fall short, those longing for compassion will usually applaud any attempts made toward comfort.

Start with Recognition

You may want to start discussions with ministry leaders at your church by educating them about the probable number of church members who are struggling with infertility. You may also want to let them know that the first step toward offering help to these hurting people is simply acknowledging to the congregation that such anguish exists. Pastors can mention the realities from the pulpit. Hospital visitation can include families reeling from stillbirth. The church can be made available as a meeting place for a Christ-centered infertility support group that is open to your community.

If the definition of *family* begins with marriage vows, then proactively addressing fertility challenges can realistically begin with premarital counseling. While about one in six couples find themselves struggling with impaired ability to conceive, not to mention the even higher odds of pregnancy loss, these families are almost always caught by surprise. Most never even consider it could actually happen to them.

If not to the body of Christ, where can families turn for counsel? There *are* many resources for families facing fertility-related crises, but few come from a God-honoring worldview. It is extremely frustrating to couples who come to their church earnestly looking for moral guidance to be met with criticism of their choices, attacks about their lack of faith, or pat answers rather than true guidance. While pastors don't have to have deep ethical insights into every possible reproductive technology available, they should be prepared to offer basic scriptural guidelines from which seeking families can make godly, life-affirming decisions. You can even offer to help your pastor compile a library of resources for this purpose.

One venue to consider in your church might be your adult Sunday school program. Many churches offer newlywed and new parent classes, with no alternatives to bridge the gap for those who are well past newlywed stage yet still waiting for parenthood.

A common answer to infertile couples is "just adopt." Adoption is not only an emotionally taxing journey that God may or may not be calling an individual family to pursue, but often a huge financial burden as well. God's charge to the entire body of Christ is "to look after orphans and widows in their distress" (James 1:27). There are many creative ways even for small congregations to help families called to the joy of adoption.

Educating the Church

Ministry leaders might need to be educated not only about the primary issues of infertility and child loss, but also about all the surrounding "baggage" that typically accompanies these heartaches, such as anger, depression, grief, intense marital stress, or physical health struggles. Heartache can sometimes seem so all-consuming that other needs are neglected. Grief isn't a one-time occurrence and is over; it's an ongoing process that needs regular attention.

The Bible is filled with barren and bereaved families. Seek the Lord's guidance as you talk with your pastor about how to address some of these stories on Sunday mornings. Ministry leaders can be gently reminded to be careful of statements such as "Children are the ultimate sign of God's blessing on your marriage" or "Motherhood (or fatherhood) is the highest calling for Christian women (or men)." These cut grieving couples to the heart.

When a church becomes family-focused to the exclusion of anyone who does not "fit the mold," many are left feeling excluded. Women's events that are primarily just moms' events are painful not only for infertile women, but also for unmarried women longing for families. Those grieving the death of any loved one, post-abortive men and women, singles, widows, those shattered by divorce, those married to unbelieving spouses, or parents whose children are not walking with the Lord all share the same feelings of exclusion in family-focused churches.

Infertile families often decry a few especially painful areas where the typical American church could use significant change in its approach. The "big three" tend to be Mother's Day, Father's Day, and baby dedications and baptisms. A few denominations also celebrate Baby Day once a year, while others put huge effort into Pro-life Sunday.

It isn't necessary to remove these events from the calendar, but churches should strive for balance. For example, a church that celebrates Baby Day should also be willing to hold a memorial service for a miscarried child. If your church has an abortion-themed service on the yearly anniversary of *Roe v. Wade*, even a brief mention of how hard this topic is for families facing the pain of infertility or loss can make this more survivable for grieving hearts.

While God's union of husband and wife in a marriage ceremony is typically held independently from worship services, baby baptisms or dedications usually take center stage on Sunday mornings. Some churches have found a wonderful compromise by moving baby dedications to their own special service (away from Sunday mornings), thus offering even more dedicated attention to the celebrating families, while giving grieving families a chance to participate only when they are emotionally able to rejoice with those who rejoice.

If dedications do need to stay in your regular service, try to limit their frequency (maybe two to four dedications yearly), don't hold them on other already emotionally charged days such as holidays, and publicize them well ahead of time. Child-focused events are more painful when they come as a surprise, especially during corporate worship. Simple communication can go a long way. Posting baby-related events in the bulletin for several weeks prior to the date allows families to prepare their hearts, to sit near the back, or even to make alternate plans for that day.

Kelley was taken by surprise when she attended church on "children's ministry day," which included baby dedications. She wrote,

> Oh boy, was I bombarded with babies and kids all around. The
> sermon was even done by the children's ministry team. As my

husband and I were sitting watching the dedication, I started to long to be one of those families up there, proud and giving thanks to God for that special blessing I've always dreamed about.

To get my mind off it I started to read the church bulletin. I saw a notice that the flowers that were placed at the altar were dedicated to the families who have lost a child or are struggling with infertility. I started to cry and praise God that the church was aware of our pain and struggle as we sit there looking at all those proud parents and kids that we pray for. . . . This was the first time that I have seen this dedication of flowers when the baby dedication day happens (only two times a year). I was proud to go to a church that remembers us forgotten mothers who have no children to hold.

Whenever a baby dies, even in an early miscarriage, an offer of a memorial service should be given to the grieving family. (Some parents may not feel the need for a public observance, but most will appreciate the choice to decline.) Katie Jane writes, "I really appreciated it when many people in the church attended Chrissie's funeral. It said that she was significant. My biggest fear was that there would be less people there than would have turned up for her baby shower."

Presentation Sunday (explained in detail at www.cedarpark.org/infertile/ and based on the concept of Mary and Joseph presenting Jesus in the temple forty days after His birth) can be a wonderful way for churches to acknowledge and minister to families longing to expand. The date for this observance is the last Sunday of January. The idea is to allow any families struggling with fertility challenges to come before their church for public prayer. No promises are made, and not everyone prayed for has a miracle baby story to tell, yet what a comfort to the families who participate in these services to be upheld in prayer.

How good and pleasant it is
when brothers live together in unity!
PSALM 133:1

It may seem that I put an extraordinary amount of focus on parenting holidays, yet I cannot strongly enough express how painful these two days can be. While the principle of honoring mothers and fathers is biblical, Mother's Day and Father's Day themselves are not spiritual in nature, such as the celebrations of Christ's birth and resurrection. It is freeing to some pastors simply to realize they are not required to put a huge emphasis on greeting-card-inspired dates.

If Mother's or Father's Days are to be recognized in the church, consider 1 Timothy 5:12: "Do not rebuke an older man harshly, but exhort him as if he were your father. Treat younger men as brothers, older women as mothers, and younger women as sisters, with absolute purity." *All* men in the church are to be honored as fathers and brothers in the Lord. *All* women as mothers and sisters. In verse 21, Timothy continues, "Do nothing out of favoritism."

Many churches ask mothers and fathers to stand for special recognition on their respective holidays. Some churches offer gifts. A few even offer awards for things like having the most kids or being the newest mom. While the intention behind this recognition is admirable, I can attest, even going into my fifth Mother's Day with living children in my home, that for those who desire to stand but are unqualified for such honor, these traditions are torturous.

After that disastrous Mother's Day that sent me spiraling into such depression, Rick and I intentionally avoided church on Mother's Day and Father's Day for the next several years. When I finally thought I would be able to face a Mother's Day church service again, I made it only as far as the giving of flowers to moms before I was sobbing. While I could have stood in acknowledgment of our child in heaven, I didn't want to risk anyone thinking

I was making a pregnancy announcement. As tears streamed down my face, an usher quietly slipped a flower in my lap during the dedication prayer. She had no way of knowing my story, or how her action blessed my heart!

I've actually heard several tear-filled stories in which infertile men or women were mistakenly given gifts on Mother's or Father's Day at their churches, only to have the token taken back when someone realized they weren't parents to living children. Other women report being handed flowers like consolation prizes with comments such as "You aren't a mom, but I guess you can have a flower anyway."

Doing nothing out of favoritism might include giving a gift to all women in your congregation, being careful to avoid the "consolation prize" mentality. One church did a beautiful job replacing their standard Mother's Day Tea with a Victorian "Day of Loveliness" (based on Philippians 4:8), filled with music, elegant food, edification, devotion and praise, open to all women. Opening your parent's day service with a heartfelt prayer for all hurting on this holiday can go a long way toward softening the sting of being left out of the celebration.

My heart rejoiced when my pastor began this year's Mother's Day sermon by reading letters from a mom who lost her teenager in a car accident and from an infertile couple. He also mentioned men and women who had lost their moms and those who had not had good moms in their lives. His sermon focused on how all people have an inborn need to be mothered and how this desire should point us to Christ, the only one who can meet every need.

For this is what the LORD says: "... As a mother comforts her child, so will I comfort you."

ISAIAH 66:12-13

For Further Thought

(When Nicolle Reece learned her son would very possibly not survive birth due to severe heart defects, her pastor provided a phone number to use whenever

the time came. She writes about what followed.)

After Micah died we had no idea what to do. I took the phone number out of my purse and told Jim to call. We didn't know who we were calling or what, if anything, they could do. Jim explained the situation and quickly hung up. He told me he had spoken with a woman named Rebecca (we had never even met her, very large congregation) and that she was making the one-and-a-half-hour drive to the hospital. She was a mortician.

I didn't know what to expect. I sat in a rocking chair holding Micah when she came into the room. She rushed over to me, took my hand, and cried. Not the half-sniffling kind, she just openly cried. She didn't say a word for over thirty minutes. I just felt this overwhelming love and caring from a total stranger; I truly feel God sent her to us. She lovingly cared for Micah and the rest of our family, helped us in making funeral arrangements and saying good-bye. This has been the most meaningful thing anyone has ever done for me. If we are ever blessed with another child and she's a girl, her name will also be Rebecca.

Our pastor was also wonderful. He arrived at the funeral home the next day, marched right up to me (I was holding Micah's body), and asked if he could hold him. I was so touched. (The majority of our friends and family at the funeral did not even look at him.) He prayed for our peace, that we would feel God's love, and thanked God for taking care of Micah. We did receive immense peace with prayer, but I was especially thankful for his gentle reminder that above all we should be thankful for the gift of eternal life and that God was truly in all ways Micah's Father.

 Heart Treasures

Psalm 1:1-2

Mark 5:25-34

James 2:1-17

1 Peter 4:8

Burden Bearers

Pastor, invite me to share my ideas with you. Families like mine can become your best resource for transforming your good intentions into constructive actions.

I fully agree with the Bible's claims that children are a blessing. I only ask that our church be aware that many of us cannot take such a gift for granted. Please don't elevate parenthood to the point where I feel cursed because I have not been so blessed.

An honest "I don't know the right thing to say or do" or simple "I'm sorry" is a great start. I don't usually want or expect to be fixed, nearly as much as I need a listening ear, a friendly hug, and lots of prayer.

When my baby dies, a care package to help meet everyday needs like milk, bread, and fruit or high-energy, ready-made food items will help remove some of the stress of little tasks that feel so huge in the face of grief, like shopping, cooking, or even eating.

Or perhaps a group such as my Bible study could coordinate a checklist of options for things I might desire such as meals, housecleaning, lawn mowing, running errands, or babysitting my living children for an hour, day, night, or weekend. From your list I can select the several options I most need.

(Visit www.hannah.org/resources/church.htm for more information and assistance.)

worshiping while waiting

She said, "May your servant find favor in your eyes." Then she went her way and ate something, and her face was no longer downcast. Early the next morning they arose and worshiped before the LORD and then went back to their home at Ramah. Elkanah lay with Hannah his wife, and the LORD remembered her.

1 SAMUEL 1:18-19

But they that wait upon the LORD shall renew their strength; they shall mount up with wings as eagles; they shall run, and not be weary; and they shall walk, and not faint.

ISAIAH 40:31 (KJV)

She had flown back to Elkanah with her heart carrying her on wings of joy, finally ready to partake in the feast. It had been so wonderful to return to the temple the next morning to worship with her husband by her side. And the trip back to Ramah had not seemed even half as long as the reverse route to Shiloh had been days before.

But now they were home. The glow of her mountain-top encounter was quickly fading. Her monthly uncleanness was due any day. Familiar anxiety was threatening to overwhelm her once again. Maybe it would have been better if she had never journeyed to Shiloh.

If this month turned out no different from all she had known before, her devastation would be magnified by the hope she had allowed to spring in her heart. After all these years of practice, she should have learned patience by now, but waiting seemed harder this month than ever before. 'Father, I need your strength! How do I find the balance between surrender and hope?'

Eli promised Hannah a baby, and she went home to conceive immediately, right? I would like to challenge this popular interpretation. First and foremost, I do not read that Eli (or God) promised Hannah a baby. While Eli was greatly compassionate toward Hannah, speaking words of blessing, ultimately he could only *ask* God to grant her heart's desire. Second, beyond knowing that Elkanah worshiped with his wife the next morning before returning home, Scripture does not spell out a clear timeline for us.

While God does promise children to some as He did for Sarah, Elizabeth, and Samson's mother, many more are like Hannah, learning to trust God without such firm knowledge of His future plans. "But hope that is seen is no hope at all," we read in Romans. "Who hopes for what he already has? But if we hope for what we do not yet have, we wait for it patiently" (8:24-25).

While I may not be able to cling to the promise of a baby, I can still find great hope by resting in God's plan. The apostle Paul wrote,

> Therefore we do not lose heart. Though outwardly we are wasting away, yet inwardly we are being renewed day by day. For our light and momentary troubles are achieving for us an eternal glory that far outweighs them all. So we fix our eyes not on what is seen, but on what is unseen. For what is seen is temporary, but what is unseen is eternal. (2 Corinthians 4:16-18)

Hannah left the temple with peace and renewed hope because she had placed her grief in the hands of her mighty God. But she left still not knowing how God would choose to act. One Bible commentator remarks, "She had by prayer committed her case to God and left it with him, and now she was no more perplexed about it. She had prayed for herself, and Eli had prayed for her; and she believed that God would either give her the mercy she had prayed for or make up the want of it to her some other way. Prayer is heart's ease to a gracious soul."[1]

By looking for favor in Eli's eyes, Hannah accepted God's sovereignty in her life. According to Bruce Wilkinson, "When we ask for God's blessings, we're not asking for more of what we could get for ourselves. We're crying out for the wonderful, unlimited goodness that only God has the power to know about or give us."[2] God is God and we are *not*. Hannah committed herself to God's best for her life, whatever that best might turn out to be.

She made a choice to leave behind her cloak of grief and take on the garments of praise. The change was tangible, unmistakable, and visible for all to see in her very countenance. There was a spring in her step, joy in her heart, undeniable strength in her straightened posture, and grace in her glowing face. Baby or no baby, her God had not forgotten her after all.

Just as God called Abraham to trust Him by offering the life of his long-awaited Isaac (see Genesis 22), He asked Hannah to place her desires sacrificially before Him. To spare Isaac's life, God provided a ram, but not until the last moment, once Isaac was bound and Abraham's knife was raised for the kill. It was only in radical obedience, placing God first in his heart even before his beloved son, that Abraham found peace.

In *A Graceful Waiting,* the best book I've ever read on the topic of waiting, Jan Frank writes, "Waiting becomes worship when our as-yet-unfulfilled hopes and dreams take a secondary place to knowing, loving, and trusting our God."[3] Surely Hannah hoped that God might "provide a ram" for her as well. But her freedom from depression came in fully trusting God's best for her life, even at the price of sacrificing her longings.

Praise Amidst Brokenness

The very first morning after her temple visit, Hannah and Elkanah began a new chapter of their lives with the conscious decision to worship the Lord.

This attitude of praise was like putting on a pair of glasses and seeing the world with new eyes. In the midst of a long struggle through infertility, my friend Alison shared, "I always find that when I start to count my blessings, praise just follows naturally. I realize just how thankful I am for the Lord and all He has done for me in Christ. Yet when I focus on my problems, I feel like He has abandoned me, and my emotions go spiraling down."

While it is easy to read Hannah's story as one event immediately following another, we only know that *sometime* after their return home, God allowed Hannah to conceive. It is quite possible they still faced a waiting season back in Ramah. Maybe God opened Hannah's womb that very first night back in Elkanah's bed . . . or maybe it was still several months or even years. At the very least, Hannah's newfound peace would have been immediately tested by the infamous two-week wait that every infertile woman dreads.

God had met her in her place of brokenness; now she had to trust Him as she waited for His plans to be revealed. The Lord brought me to this point of decision as well:

Lord, help me to *know* that You are enough. Take my eyes off myself. Take my eyes off the child I desire. Help me to delight myself in You. Mold the desires of my heart to be in line with Your will. I don't want to *need* to be a mother more than I need to be your humble, obedient child. I don't want wanting to have a baby to be a stumbling block between You and me anymore.

Lord, I want to give this desire, this drive, this ache up to You. Help me not to snatch it back as I so often do with the burdens I place in Your hands. Help me to be *truly* content with Your will and Your timing.

Lord, You know that I still desire a baby — someone to mold, teach, train, shape, guide, and help to grow in You. But until the day You give me that joyous blessing, help *me* to grow in You. Let me reach out to those around me. Let me witness and minister to the children You place in my path.

Lord, if adoption is the path You would have us take, prepare our hearts, and prepare the child who will share our home. If adoption is not Your will for our lives, keep me from pushing ahead of Your plan. Help me to stay submitted to my husband's will, and to Your will. If we are headed in the wrong direction, change our hearts.

Thank You for lifting my burden. Help me to keep You first! Let me seek Your face daily, and let me know that *You are enough!*[4]

This was my prayer of brokenness. It was my prayer of learning to let God be God in my life. It was the beginning of relinquishing my "right" to motherhood and of seeking hard after God's fatherhood in my heart. It was my recognition that God is *worthy* of my worship and that my praise should not be contingent upon the gifts He gives or chooses to withhold. I eagerly await the chance to meet Hannah one day in heaven to compare notes, for I suspect her own prayers may have been much the same.

Was life suddenly free of pain when Hannah learned to worship God in the interludes of life? If she was like me, the answer is a resounding "Yes! And no!"

Yes in that a huge burden was lifted. Hannah no longer felt responsible to earn God's favor for the blessing of a child. Having a baby no longer seemed dependent on convincing God that He should send one. *Yes* in that *my* heart was healing, being filled by a hunger for the Lord like I had never known before.

No for us both, in that our arms were still empty, our realities unchanged, our want still very real. And, at least for me, my human nature often continued getting in the way, temporarily causing me to forget God's hard-earned place on my heart's throne. It was another five and a half years from the week God brought me to my knees in submission until the afternoon we brought home our newborn son, a day I had no way of knowing would ever come.

My surrender started with the breaking of my heart, of my will. Relinquishment was a conscious, painful decision. Learning to worship through the wait was not a one-time event, but an ongoing process. Many times through those years I questioned God and struggled. But finally my heart was, overall, headed in the right direction. I was taking at least one or two steps forward for every step backward, instead of the other way around.

Restore to me the joy of your salvation
and grant me a willing spirit, to sustain me.
PSALM 51:12

As Russell Kelfer so well expressed in one of my all-time favorite poems, "Wait," below, I often wished I could see enough of God's plan at least to know if the battle was even worth such grief. If only God would tell me, "Yes, someday you will have a baby," or even "No, my plans for you do not include a child," then I would have either been able to rest in the peace of knowing or grieve my losses and move on.

Living in the ongoing unknown made worship a true sacrifice. Blind faith was sometimes fearful, painful faith, especially whenever I tried to exercise it in my own strength. Fortunately, each time I made even the meekest attempt to reach out to the Lord, my Father was there to hold my hand and guide me along the way.

Wait

Desperately, helplessly, longingly, I cried.
Quietly, patiently, lovingly, He replied.
I pleaded, and I wept for a clue to my fate,
And the Master so gently said, "Child, you must wait."

"Wait? Your say wait?" my indignant reply.
"Lord, I need answers, I need to know why.
Is your hand shortened? Or have you not heard?
By faith I have asked, and I'm claiming your Word.

"My future, and all to which I can relate
Hangs in the balance, and you tell me 'wait'?
I'm needing a 'yes,' a go-ahead sign,
Or even a 'no,' to which I can resign.

"And Lord, you have promised that if we believe,
We need but to ask, and we shall receive.
And Lord I've been asking, and this is my cry:
I'm weary of asking: I need a reply!"

Then quietly, softly, I learned of my fate
As my Master replied once again, "You must wait."
So I slumped in my chair; defeated and taut
And grumbled to God; "So I'm waiting, for what?"

He seemed then to kneel and His eyes met with mine
And He tenderly said, "I could give you a sign.
I could shake the heavens, darken the sun,
Raise the dead, cause the mountains to run.

"All you see I could give, and pleased you would be.
You would have what you want, but you wouldn't know Me.
You'd not know the depth of My love for each saint;
You'd not know the power that I give to the faint.

"You'd not learn to see through clouds of despair;
You'd not learn to trust, just by knowing I'm there.

You'd not know the joy of resting in Me,
When darkness and silence was all you could see.

"You would never experience that fullness of love
As the peace of My Spirit descends like a dove.
You would know that I give, and I save, for a start,
But you'd not know the depth of the beat of My heart.

"The glow of My comfort late in the night;
The faith that I give when you walk without sight;
The depth that's beyond getting just what you ask
From an infinite God who makes what you have last.

"And you never would know, should your pain quickly flee,
What it means that 'My grace is sufficient for thee.'
Yes, your dreams for that loved one o'ernight could come true,
But the loss! if you lost what I'm doing in you.

"So be silent, my child, and in time you will see
That the greatest of gifts is to get to know Me.
And though oft' may My answers seem terribly late,
My most precious answer of all . . . is still . . . wait."[5]

For Further Thought
(From "Fear of the Unknown" by Ginger Garrett)

Our suffering can increase through the agony of not knowing when it will end and why God has allowed it. We want answers to questions that God does not seem eager to explain. . . . We imagine that if only God would tell us the day and time that our wait will end, we could relax and pace ourselves during our waiting.

But the idea that this suffering could stretch on indefinitely haunts us and makes the present much more difficult. We can stand short bursts of pain, such as in the dentist's chair or when we get a flu shot, because we know the pain will end quickly and because we feel confident the suffering will produce a greater good. We don't seem to need or ask for God's strength in those moments. . . .

Lack of control, however, with no sense of when the suffering will end or why God allows it, nudges us to an all-knowing, all-powerful Lord. God can best demonstrate who He is when we are paying careful attention. Perhaps this is one reason why He does not reveal to us His exact times and dates and reasons. We want Him to reveal the future — He wants to reveal His character.[6]

Heart Treasures

Genesis 22:1-18

Psalm 27:14

Psalm 40

Isaiah 61:3

Romans 12:1-2

Colossians 3:2

Hebrews 13:15

Burden Bearers

While I'm waiting, please don't ask me if I'm pregnant yet each time you see me. While I appreciate the loving support, your constant reminders can cause me to become more discontent with God's timing.

in the course of time

So in the course of time Hannah conceived and gave birth to
a son. She named him Samuel, saying, "Because I asked the
LORD for him."
1 SAMUEL 1:20

He settles the barren woman in her home
as a happy mother of children.
Praise the LORD.
PSALM 113:9

*While there had been a season of letdown after her trip to Shiloh,
Hannah was amazed at the overall peace that ruled her heart these
days. Loneliness had been eclipsed by hope. Lack of direction, replaced
by purpose. As time marched on, 'grace' seemed to best sum up the
experience.*

*She would forever remain in awe that the God she once feared
would care for her in such a personal manner. The realization that He
lovingly made Himself available to any who truly sought after Him
caused Hannah to mourn for the spiritual decay of her countrymen.
He readily drew close to the brokenhearted, and yet there seemed so
few human prospects for the revival of Israel.*

*As she grappled with the desire to spread hope to those around her,
she was drawn to a recent figure in her nation's history. What wisdom*

this prophetess possessed, that the songs called Deborah 'a mother of Israel' (Judges 5:7)! It was Hannah's constant prayer that God would raise up another leader to parent the Jews back to His heart.

Sometimes there isn't a storybook ending like Hannah's. Several of my friends are medically sterile. Others have never married or are single again after divorce or widowhood; though the longing for children is strong, they have no means to act on their desires. Many are still waiting for God's final plans to be revealed, hopeful that His path for them will include children, yet uncertain of His timing or outcome. And then there are the mothers whose children all live in heaven.

While you may have identified with Hannah's story quite a bit so far, if you haven't conceived and given birth, your ability to relate to this woman may seem over. But before you toss this chapter aside, please hang in here with me a little longer.

We started our journey into the depths of Hannah's heart by finding a working definition of *family*. Let's now consider what it means to be a *mother*. Webster's definition includes the following: "a female parent; a woman in authority; the superior of a religious community of women; an elderly woman; maternal tenderness or affection; of, relating to, or being a mother; bearing the relation of a mother; to give birth to; to give rise to; to care for or protect like a mother."[1] Wow! Motherhood has to do with a lot more than just the physical act of giving birth or even of raising a child.

I debated about the use of Psalm 113:9 as an opening verse here. And then one day on the childlessnotbychoice.com message boards, I noticed that the New King James rendition replaces *as* with *like*: "He settles the barren woman in her home *like* a happy mother of children" (emphasis added). God wants to make me content, fully satisfying my longings. If He does not do so through traditional motherhood, His better plan can bring joy in every way equal to the fulfillment I seek in children.

Sometimes God's definitions are outside my preconceived notions.

Psalm 103 assures us that the Lord does satisfy desires. How? With "good things" (verse 5). God's good is never second best.

Those fears about not having children and grandchildren to care for you in your old age are understandable, and yet God has not overlooked this detail. "God sets the lonely in families" (Psalm 68:6) and will meet even this need. One of the benefits of walking with the Lord is your membership in an extended "family of believers" (Galatians 6:10).

"Last week one of my coworkers had a miscarriage," Jan writes.

> Since I've never been pregnant, I really didn't know how to relate to her. But thanks be to God and the advice of my wonderful "sisters" from Hannah's Prayer, I sent her an e-mail this morning and we spent time sharing our thoughts with one another over an extended break. I don't know if I will ever be able to join in the club of "motherhood," but I sure get a joy out of being able to be a blessing to someone else and getting my mind off me and my problems. I feel like God showered me with a fresh rain.

I truly understand Jan's longings to be part of "the club of motherhood." During my childless years I found the most solace in my circle of friends who had also experienced fertility challenges. Yet sometimes even this support became painful. It seemed that every time I grew really close to a new friend, she immediately adopted or got pregnant. There were a couple of especially isolating years when Rick and I were the only members of Hannah's Prayer leadership who were not parents to living children. I felt singled out as "infertile even among the infertile."

What I didn't see for a long time was that Jan's story, along with my own, already painted beautiful pictures of motherhood. No baby involved, no giving birth, no children in our homes, and yet we were mothers to other hurting hearts. Like Hannah, we each had a mother's heart even without little hearts to mother.

I've often been bothered by all the passages telling me to teach the Lord's ways to my children. If I do not have them, how can I apply these verses? Psalm 78 gave me a new perspective:

> We will not hide them from *their* children;
>   we will tell the next generation
> the praiseworthy deeds of the LORD,
>   his power, and the wonders he has done. . . .
> Then they would put their trust in God"
>
> (VERSES 4-7, EMPHASIS ADDED)

Motherhood can mean asking God to allow me the joy of passing His love on to future generations, even if I am not technically their mother.

The Amplified Bible specifies that the barren women can become a "joyful mother of [spiritual] children" (Psalm 113:9). Are you anyone's mentor (a child's, a teenager's, even an adult's)? Is there a little one on your block who knows she can always knock on your door and find a playmate, listener, storyteller, game-player, or chocolate-chip-cookie-baker? Are you a mother at your church, filling that niche that God has carved out just for you in Sunday school, choir, hospitality, or some other ministry? Do you give of yourself as a daughter to other mothers by visiting the elderly who have no family at all? *Mom* often goes by the synonym *friend*.

God's view of my value is further confirmed by Jesus' response to a woman in the crowd who called out to Him: "'Blessed is the mother who gave you birth and nursed you.' He replied, 'Blessed rather are those who hear the word of God and obey it'" (Luke 11:27-28). The Lord puts much more importance on eternal relationships than on earthly ones.

In *Safe in the Arms of God,* John MacArthur writes, "God's desire for each of us, not just expectant mothers, is that we will understand that He and He alone is the author and finisher of our lives. He is the One who gives us our identity, our value, and our sense of belonging. He alone is the One who makes us whole and raises us up to maturity in the image of Christ Jesus."[2]

Peter reminds us,

> For this very reason, make every effort to add to your faith goodness; and to goodness, knowledge; and to knowledge, self-control; and to self-control, perseverance; and to perseverance, godliness; and to godliness, brotherly kindness; and to brotherly kindness, love. For if you possess these qualities in increasing measure, they will keep you from being ineffective and unproductive in your knowledge of our Lord Jesus Christ.
>
> (2 PETER 1:5-8)

These verses really hit home when you consider the wording of the King James translation, where "ineffective and unproductive" are replaced with "barren nor unfruitful." God wants my *heart* to be fertile soil for His love to blossom, even if my *womb* remains ever barren.

> *"Sing, O barren woman, you who never bore a child; burst into song, shout for joy, you who were never in labor; because more are the children of the desolate woman than of her who has a husband," says the LORD.*
>
> ISAIAH 54:1

If you are feeling unprepared to read reflections related to successful adoption, pregnancy (including loss and live birth), or child-rearing, jump to the For Further Thought section near the end of this chapter now.

Dreams Fulfilled

While the years of Hannah's barrenness had seemed agonizingly long, these brief months to cherish her beloved miracle had flashed by in the blink of an eye. It was bittersweet to inspect the creeping roadside critters with her three-year-old son, then take his hand for the remainder of their journey to Shiloh. Hannah worried about how Samuel would feel this first night in a strange place without her.

And after the sheltering protection of home, she struggled over the moral decay to which he would suddenly be exposed. While the temple should provide a safe place for her little boy to grow closer to God, trusting Eli with his care was a huge step of faith, considering how the priest's own boys had turned their backs on the Lord.

How she would need God's strength for the lonely walk home! She clung to the hope that, as He had enabled her to survive a hollow womb, the Lord would surely help her cope with empty arms once again. As she forced her mind to remember His goodness, her heart began to compose a song:

> *My heart rejoices in the LORD. . . .*

> *There is no one holy like the LORD;*
>   *there is no one besides you;*
>   *there is no Rock like our God. . . .*

> *She who was barren has borne seven children,*
>   *but she who has had many sons pines away.*
>   (1 SAMUEL 2:1-10)

There are unique joys and struggles that come only when long-awaited desires are fulfilled. One legacy of fertility challenges is the loss of the innocence of thinking babies "just happen." Ecclesiastes 1:18 states it well: "For with much wisdom comes much sorrow; the more knowledge, the more grief." Whether you have experienced prior loss or simply know too much from reading, researching, and watching others' tragedies, a new pregnancy or adoption journey can be filled with emotional land mines.

If God's will does lead you to traditional parenthood, your parenting years may yet continue to be impacted by your reproductive history. The first conflicted emotions begin as you contemplate how to share your news with friends who have shared your journey. You have been on the "left behind" side of so many parenthood announcements, and now you are in the position to cause the same pain.

Raising a child can be overwhelming under any circumstances, but entering child-rearing via fertility challenges tends to set families up for unrealistic expectations. After so many years to romanticize and build up the experience in your mind, the realities sometimes bring disillusionment. The morning sickness or pregnancy complications you swore you would welcome without complaint may tax your emotions even more than your body. Growing your family from two to four or more overnight, through multiple birth or sibling adoption, can take an especially hard toll.

Sleep deprivation, the exhausting and demanding needs accompanying a premature birth, having your family routine turned inside-out by "instant" parenthood through adoption — none of these may mesh with your dreams. Keep in mind that these days of trial are a brief season. While every twenty-four hours may seem unending right now, in the grand scheme of things, they will pass much too quickly. Look again to Psalm 113:9, asking the Lord to keep you truly joyful in your parenting.

Calling your infertile friends to complain about parenting struggles isn't fair, but looking for support from those who haven't been there may well land you the unsympathetic response, "You asked for this." Carefully select a support network, such as the motherhood forums on the Hannah's Prayer message boards, where you can find daily encouragement. Do not try to carry the burden of "perfect parenthood" all alone.

Just as there were no guarantees in fertility challenges, there are no guarantees in parenting. Sometimes long-awaited children turn their backs on the Lord. This too is part of Hannah's experience. Her own grandchildren, sons of the prophet Samuel, chose an ungodly path (see 1 Samuel 8). God

Himself, the only truly perfect parent, has many prodigal children. While we pour our hearts and prayers into our kids and do all in our power to protect them physically and spiritually, we must ultimately entrust their life choices to our Father.

Just as Hannah offered Samuel back to the Lord, we must continually place our beloved charges in His care. This was never clearer to me than during the five-day vigil at my son's hospital bedside the week before his first birthday. What started as slight sniffles and fussiness, in less than twenty-four hours became a menacing infection threatening to cross the barrier from his eye to his brain.

As I watched my baby hooked up to tubes and monitors, and pumped full of several strong medications, I wondered if God would call him home only a year after entrusting him to our care. As I wrestled and pleaded for my son's life, the Lord gently asked, "Can you trust Me?" Lessons learned through infertility served me well in this new crisis.

Fear wasn't new territory. It had been my biggest struggle the entire nine months I carried Joshua. Seven years of nothing but "failure" had programmed my heart to guard against hope. Toward the end of the pregnancy, my mom even asked me in exasperation, "Are you ever going to accept the fact that everything is fine? When talking about this baby's birth, you always say *if* and never *when*." That "when" didn't come until I was pushing him out of my body and was taken by the joyful surprise that we had actually made it to live birth. Then, for the next year, I found myself continually interrupting my poor child's sleep in fear of SIDS.

Satan knew my weak points well. It didn't seem to matter what landmark I'd reached; that week I was flooded with e-mails and phone calls from other women who had experienced loss at my exact stage of pregnancy. Some called in fresh grief while other shared stories from years prior, but the Stealer of Joy coordinated the timing of their contacts to feed my fears.

The sword of the Spirit, God's Word, was my best defense against the Enemy's attacks. I would meditate by the hour over Philippians 4:6-8, listing on paper all I could think of that was true, noble, right, pure, lovely, admirable, excellent, or praiseworthy about my pregnancy. While Job's story was devastating, it also comforted me to realize that Satan could do nothing to me or my baby without asking God's permission first.

For you did not receive a spirit that makes you a slave again to fear, but you received the Spirit of sonship [adoption]. And by him we cry, "Abba, Father."

ROMANS 8:15

The Journey Continues

Out of the thousands of infertile adoptive families I've been blessed to meet, I personally know only a few dozen to whom the Lord has later given biological children. And of these I can think of just five or six "surprises," while the rest were actively sought conceptions. (I know many more surprises whose older siblings were born via aggressive medical aid, but these joyful miracles receive far less public attention than post-adoption conceptions.)

For every one pregnancy-after-adoption story out there, hundreds of people may hear the news and find ammunition to fire against another weary infertile family: "Just adopt, then you'll get pregnant." Adoptive moms who do get pregnant almost always hear, "See, I told you so," and often feel guilty for perpetuating the myth. Adoption is a beautiful path in and of itself and should never be viewed as a means to the end of getting pregnant.

Proverbs states that the barren womb "never says, 'Enough!'" (30:16). While many women battling infertility yearn for "just one" baby, if you ask these same women what their family hopes had looked like prior to fertility challenges, they typically admit to having always dreamed of *children* (plural, not singular). Bringing home a child via birth or adoption does not end the infertility journey, either physically or emotionally, for many families.

Because it had taken us seven years to have Joshua, we started actively "trying" again when he was just six weeks old. The technical name for the next phase of our journey is "secondary infertility." We went into round two prepared that it might be a battle. I frequently asked the Lord if we hadn't paid our dues during our first seven years. I didn't want to become so consumed by the quest for additional children that I squandered time with our son, but in reality that is exactly what happened sometimes.

First-time infertility is always a painful surprise. While secondary infertility was a hard journey, we were thankful for coping skills learned through our primary years. We had a definite emotional advantage over friends who had previously grown their families with ease but then floundered in the dark waters of conception- and pregnancy-failure.

I knew from personal experience that a baby in the waiting room of a fertility clinic was cruel irony. Unfortunately, my body didn't stop having problems just because I had given birth. Now I found myself trying to manage raging endometriosis and cope through two miscarriages, while the casual waiting-room observer could only see a carefree young mom.

I was now a biological mother, but I still didn't emotionally fit in that "club of motherhood" I had so yearned to qualify for. I came home from my first Mothers of Preschoolers meeting in tears, feeling like a total impostor. The old infertility viper struck my heart as friends confidently planned out the months and seasons of future conceptions or bemoaned ineffective birth-control methods.

As my baby grew up before my eyes, great joy was mixed with the grief of thinking this would likely be my "only chance" and wishing to savor every fleeting moment. The longing for another baby intensified with each passed milestone, and yet these desires were tempered with guilt that I shouldn't want more after receiving such a blessing, when so many remained without a child at all. In retrospect, I now realize that I missed out on many of the joys of Joshua's first years simply because my heart still "felt infertile" and couldn't really reconcile the reality of God's gift of a child with the pain of seven previous years.

The day my two-year-old said his first independent prayer, "Jesus, Joshua please baby sister. Joshua want brother," was my undoing. The emotions of infertility hit with full force all over again. While it was Joshua's desire for a sibling that crystallized our second infertility experience, it was our third child who launched me into the all-too-familiar emotions to begin with. My journal explains how I was impacted by Joel's death, shortly after Joshua's first birthday:

> I don't think I would be "feeling infertile" so early in the game this time, had it not been for this loss. With Noel, our sorrow was finally culminating in a baby we could call by name, even if we could not hold her in our arms. She brought hope and joy because we were finally parents after two long, hard years.
>
> In contrast, this time we were willing to get pregnant and excited at the thought of another child, but with Joshua so new and such a delight to fill our empty home, we were not feeling the same urgency to conceive. Having to say good-bye before we could say hello, I'm plunged headlong into the transition from simply being willing to get pregnant to actually grieving my inability to conceive again.

Hannah followed Joel to heaven about three and a half months later. I still get angry when I think of sitting in a doctor's office, talking with him about the *pregnancy* and *miscarriage*. Yet when I mentioned my *baby*, I was quickly informed that he "wouldn't call it a baby. It was only a chemical pregnancy." I was livid. I left the office in tears and only returned once, to pick up my medical records to transfer to a new office.

For families with living children, the inability to conceive or the death of a child is often minimized with "Be thankful for your other kids." While we are abundantly thankful, the parable of the good shepherd points out the value of *every* life. If He would leave ninety-nine to look for one lost sheep, then my grief over this missing child is indeed valid.

Unlike marriage, a bond only until your spouse's death, you will remain your baby's mother for the rest of your life. *Grieving the Child I Never Knew*, written by four-time bereaved mother Kathe Wunnenberg, helped me work through the heartache of my back-to-back losses. I highly recommend this book to any woman who has ever lost a child at any stage of pregnancy or early infancy.

I deeply analyzed and struggled with questions about the eternal destiny of my miscarried children. John MacArthur writes, "Many people are quickly assured and temporarily comforted by the statement 'Your baby is in heaven.' Others are not. An explanation for *why* this is true is critical for them and, long-term, even for the superficially comforted."[3] My reading of MacArthur's book, *Safe in the Arms of God*, was at the worthwhile cost of many tears to find encouraging, biblically sound answers, which reassured me of my children's place in heaven.

While there are fears and struggles, there is also incredible joy that comes with successful adoption or pregnancy and live birth after so many years of waiting. I think I must have given my nurse permanent hearing loss when she called to give me my positive pregnancy test results. I then dropped to my knees and sobbed out tears of thanksgiving and rejoicing. If we are ever privileged to someday add a child to our family through adoption, I know receiving "the call" will be just as amazing on that day.

After having lost Noel before we had a chance to ever make a pregnancy announcement, I resolved to treasure every moment we were given with future children. Even if pregnancies were short-lived, I didn't want to live with regrets over not having enjoyed each baby for whatever time we had. While some prefer to guard their news in fear of miscarriage, I wanted to tell everyone as quickly as possible so that if I did miscarry, at least our children's life would have been celebrated.

I had tough pregnancies from the physical standpoint. With Joshua there was early bleeding (possible loss of a twin) and continual vomiting, causing me to lose twelve pounds when I should have been gaining. Ruth, our surprise second living miracle, sent me to bed for eleven weeks of preterm contractions. Even so, I loved being pregnant, especially for all the firsts of wearing maternity clothes, feeling movement, and tummy pats from strangers in the store. Rick would walk into the bathroom sympathetically to rub my back or offer me ice chips, only to find me grinning from ear to ear and saying, "We're having a baby!"

Joy Mixed with Tears

All moms love and appreciate their kids, but perhaps the wonder and joy of parenthood that comes in the course of time is especially sweet. Yes, I get tired and frustrated and grumpy just like every mom, but I believe I notice the little things and really enjoy my kids more than a lot of friends who take reproduction for granted.

One day a friend and I met at the mall with our miracle babies. As we fluttered into the children's photo studio with our toddlers in strollers and my friend obviously expecting her second child, a woman walked by, averting her eyes. But not before we both saw "that look" on her face. We wanted to run to her and shout, "We are infertile too!" She had no way to know our histories, and we could only guess at hers, but how our hearts and prayers went out to her as we remembered the pain.

Last Mother's Day my four-year-old found me crying, and I tried to explain to him that I was sad for all my friends who wanted to be moms. He immediately asked God to help all the "mommies without their children." When I shared this prayer with a friend, she said it ministered to her to be thought of and prayed for as a "mommy" by any child. I pray that Joshua always maintains this sensitivity.

A common complaint among infertile and bereaved moms is that their friends who go on to parent living children after fertility challenges can sometimes become more insensitive than the general population. While we, of all people, should know better, it is as if we develop amnesia when our lives so radically change. Perhaps the pain was so hard we don't want to let our hearts go back there.

God designed manna to spoil within one or two days, yet to Moses he said, "Take an omer of manna and keep it for the generations to come, so they can see the bread I gave you to eat in the desert when I brought you out of Egypt" (Exodus 16:32). Without reminders of their heartache, His people would quickly forget the significance of their blessings. It is important that I never forget the pain and process that brought me to today's joy.

———

Be careful that you do not forget the LORD, who brought you
out of Egypt, out of the land of slavery.
DEUTERONOMY 6:12

———

For Further Thought
(From "A Spiritual Mom" by Judy Gann)

Mother's Day dawned bright and beautiful — for everyone but me. I drove into the church parking lot, turned off the ignition and sat immobile, my hands gripping the steering wheel. *Lord, I can't do this.* For seven years I'd avoided this moment.

I always wanted to be a mother. As a young girl happily playing house with my baby sister and my dolls, I dreamed of the day when I'd have my own children.

Yet as the years passed I remained single. A children's librarian, I focused my mothering capacities on the children who populated my world every day. I treasured time spent with my niece and nephew.

For many years I also experienced the blessing of mentoring several young women from my church. Surrounded by children at the library and the girls I mentored, I shoved the issue of having children on the back shelf of my mind. Until, in my early forties, I had a hysterectomy.

I was blindsided by the cavernous void in my life following surgery. The finality of the hysterectomy and the emptiness of my childless state seared my mind. Aching with inner pain, the sight of babies in the grocery store, at church, and even in the library ignited my sense of loss. Waves of grief, anger, and despair assaulted me. I plummeted into a deep depression.

In time, with the help of a compassionate counselor, I realized my sense of worth and value to God and others isn't based on motherhood, but rather on my relationship with the Lord.

But one last piece of pain remained. I refused to attend church on Mother's Day. It was easier to stay away.

Then at a women's retreat I listened intently as Jeanne spoke about attending the first Mother's Day church service after her mother's death. Single at the time, she told of the unexpected comfort she'd found at church that morning and, yes, even the tears she needed to shed. I recognized myself in her words. I thought to myself, if Jeanne can do it, maybe I can do it.

Now after seven years, I'd made it as far as the church parking lot.

Conflicting emotions battled within me as my reluctant legs carried me across the parking lot and into the church foyer. Once inside, I froze at the sight of children handing a flower to each mother. I stepped back, ready to bolt out the door.

Austin, a boy from my preschool storytime group, shyly approached with a carnation. "No thank you, Austin," I whispered. "I'm not a mother."

My eyes flooded with tears. Yet with an inner strength and calm from God alone, I turned to walk up the stairs to the sanctuary. Suddenly I felt an arm across my shoulders. I turned and gazed with blurry eyes into the face of Barbara, the mother of one of the young women I'd mentored.

"Judy," she said in a soft but firm voice. "You are a mother. You're Carla's spiritual mother." Barbara waved to Austin who returned with his fistful of flowers. My hand shook as I took the flower Austin held out to me.

For the first time I realized the word *mother* can be defined in many ways. I will never give birth to a child. But as a spiritual mother I have the rich privilege of nurturing and influencing the children and young people God places in my life. A meal with my niece and nephew and an afternoon with one of the young women in my Bible study offer precious opportunities for spiritual mothering.

Joy replaced grief as I settled in for my first Mother's Day service in many years.[4]

Heart Treasures

Deuteronomy 4:9

1 Samuel 1:27-28

2 Kings 4:27-28

Proverbs 14:10

Psalm 40:1-3

Isaiah 49:20-21

Isaiah 56:4-5

Isaiah 65:17-20

Habakkuk 3:17-18

John 19:26-27

1 Timothy 1:2

Titus 1:4

Burden Bearers

Just because I'm not a mother by traditional definition, please don't discount my thoughts with statements such as "You don't understand because you're not a mom."

Many parents experience empty nest syndrome when their children leave home. My involuntary childlessness carries many of the same emotions and struggles to find my place in a life much different from the one I always envisioned.

Intended encouragement such as "Well, at least you know you can get pregnant now" or "You can always have another one" are not comforting in the face of loss. Would you say to a widow, "Don't worry. You can always get married again"?

While I don't want you to push adoption at me, I do want your support if adoption is an avenue we end up pursuing. Our adopted children are our "real" children, not God's backup plan. We will love and cherish every child God brings into our family, their status as equal family members not dependent on how they join our lives.

If I am blessed to experience any form of traditional parenthood, please don't make me feel that my journey to child-rearing negates my prerogative to be a "real mom" with normal reactions to stress and exhaustion. I need your encouragement and support in my years of mothering just as much as I needed your love during the journey here.

hannah's prayer ministries

Praise be to the God and Father of our Lord Jesus Christ,
the Father of compassion and the God of all comfort, who
comforts us in all our troubles, so that we can comfort those in
any trouble with the comfort we ourselves have received from
God. For just as the sufferings of Christ flow over into our
lives, so also through Christ our comfort overflows.

2 CORINTHIANS 1:3-5

He who goes out weeping,
carrying seed to sow,
will return with songs of joy,
carrying sheaves with him.

PSALM 126:6

When I was broken and afraid, God used my husband to place in my hands
The Ache for a Child, a resource that is now out of print. Its author, Debra
Bridwell, has become a true mentor, mother, and friend to me. I credit her
candid exploration of infertility's realities with literally saving my life. Through
the pages of her book, God redirected my thoughts from suicide to remind me
that He loves me even in the midst of grief.

Debbie's description of an infertility support ministry at her church
sparked the desire to find such a group for myself. How I longed for such sweet
fellowship with other women who understood the entire experience of being

an infertile Christian woman. Mother's Day week of 1994, God planted in my heart the vision that He could use me to touch other hurting hearts.

Because I had been so deeply depressed, Rick initially (very wisely) advised me to wait to start such an outreach. By Thanksgiving he had witnessed God's profound and lasting transformation of my heart. We agreed that hope-based support needed to be attainable by any seeking family. The design of a beautiful logo depicting a woman praying inside a womb was Rick's answer that we could move forward with starting Hannah's Prayer Ministries.

The ministry officially launched on January 1, 1995. What we envisioned as a small gathering of couples casually meeting in our living room once a month, God planned to make into something abundantly more than all we could ask or imagine. When we asked the Christian infertility newsletter *Stepping Stones* to announce our little group, they advertised us as a support network, and letters from all over the country began filling our mailbox. When Rick decided to set up a website and e-mail address in early 1996, worldwide contacts rained in. (You can visit Hannah's Prayer Ministries at www.hannah.org.)

Shortly after Hannah's Prayer Ministries (HP) established an online presence, Julie Donahue wrote to tell me of Ladies In Waiting (LIW), the e-mail group she had formed for infertile Christian women. LIW seemed to be the Internet equivalent to all God was doing through our support groups and newsletter.

Through the years God has refined both organizations. In 2001 LIW was incorporated under the umbrella of HP. The ministry merger was finalized with the creation of our Community Forums message boards offering about eighty specialized forums for every stage and season of the journey through fertility challenges. Julie and I have gradually taken steps away from intensive hands-on leadership, while God has faithfully provided new generations of women (and a few brave men) to take over the mothering of these unified ministries.

Last year a woman named Joanie got on the Internet in the isolation of her small European island and typed "Christian support infertility" into a search engine. She later told us,

> The best I was hoping for was a book or a newsletter. You can imagine my delight when the Hannah's Prayer site came up! At a time when I seriously doubted His very existence because the pain was too senseless to bear, ladies I never met reached out to me again and again in comfort and support. They are proof to me that God *is* good. Who else could fuel so much love and generosity in people I have never even seen face to face?

Several different words in Scripture are translated as the one English word *hope*. Of these, I love the word picture painted by the hope represented by *an attached cord*. When I have this kind of hope in God, I am tethered to Him, dependent on Him. As I turn to other believers and we carry each other's burdens, the pain of isolation is removed from our hearts. Sharing such hope is what HP is all about, often becoming to our members a source of deepest friendships and sweetest fellowship.

Heather, who describes her anger and heartache as "hitting rock bottom," says,

> I was straightening up our condo and came across [our denomination's] monthly publication. On the front cover was a couple and the article was about their journey through infertility and the church. Ironically, I was about to throw the magazine away when the headline caught my eye. I read the article, and at the end, the woman listed some infertility resources. One of them was Hannah's Prayer. I joined right away, and I must say that it saved my life. It saved me spiritually, mentally, and physically.

Just when I thought I couldn't go any lower, all of these strangers began to pray for me. When I couldn't give the problems over to God myself, HP members united in prayer and lifted them off of my shoulders for me. I immediately started to feel better, and although [our fertility challenges] continued, there was comfort in knowing that I was not alone and that I had an army of prayer partners from around the world. I recommend HP to many people. I don't know where my dear husband and I would be without it.

Two are better than one, because they have a good return for their work: If one falls down, his friend can help him up. . . . A cord of three strands is not quickly broken.

ECCLESIASTES 4:9-12

A Purpose for Heartache

Hannah was a common woman with a simple dream. She wasn't expecting God to do anything big with her life; she just longed for motherhood and took her grief to the only One who could meet her needs. As she learned to worship God in the interludes of life, she began to reap the fruit of her years of heartbreak in a closer relationship with her Father. What would she have thought if someone had told her that God would choose to record her life and desires for all generations to come?

As with Hannah, this journey that began as one of the most painful, isolating experiences of my life has become a defining part of the beauty God is unfolding within me (see Psalm 119:22-24). As Jan Frank wrote in *A Graceful Waiting*, "The fruitfulness of the waiting season is hidden from us when we are in the midst of it. Trees and plants seem to be almost dead in winter. But the long winter is part of the overall plan for harvest time."[1] How might God want to bring purpose from *your* heartache? Will you give this journey fully over to Him?

resources

Author's Resources

www.hannah.org
   Hannah's Prayer Ministries, founded by Jennifer Saake. Christian
   support for infertility, pregnancy loss, infant death, and adoption.

www.jennifer.saake.biz
   Jennifer Saake's interests, favorite links, articles, family, and fun.

Infertility

The Infertility Companion and *When Empty Arms Become a Heavy Burden*
by Sandra Glahn Th.M. and William Cutrer M.D.
   Christian-centered answers to medical, ethical, emotional, marital,
   spiritual, and biblical questions raised by infertility.
   www.aspire2.com

When the Cradle Is Empty by John and Sylvia Van Regenmorter
   The Van Regenmorters direct Stepping Stones, a Christ-centered
   ministry for couples facing fertility challenges or pregnancy loss.
   www.bethany.org/step

Rain Dance by Joy DeKok
   Insightful fiction work focusing on the feelings of an infertile Christian

woman and how she copes with a friend's abortion.
www.joydekok.com

The Ache for a Child* by Debra Bridwell
Offers emotional, spiritual, and ethical insights for women suffering
through infertility and pregnancy loss.

Empty Womb, Aching Heart by Marlo Schalesky
Personal stories of women facing infertility. Hope, understanding, and
comfort.
www.marloschalesky.com

Moments for Couples Who Long for Children by Ginger Garrett
Daily devotional for the infertility journey.
www.gingergarrett.com

Taking Charge of Your Fertility by Toni Weschler
One of the few non-Christian resources you will find in my
recommendations. I do object to some of the information presented in
this book, such as categorizing abortion with other "office procedures";
however, the information on understanding and improving
reproductive health is the best I've found.
www.ovusoft.com

Pregnancy Loss or Infant Death

Grieving the Child I Never Knew by Kathe Wunnenberg
An outstanding devotional journal for surviving the loss of your
unborn or newly born child. Also by Kathe, *Grieving the Loss of a
Loved One* and *Longing for a Child*.
www.hopelifters.com

Safe in the Arms of God by John MacArthur
Theological answers about the death of a child.

A Rose in Heaven by Dawn Waltman and several contributors, including Jennifer Saake
Personal reflections on stillbirth and miscarriage.
www.remember.theroses.com

Empty Arms by Pam Vredevelt
Emotional support for those who have suffered a miscarriage, stillbirth, or tubal pregnancy. (Be sure you look for this author specifically, as this author writes from a strong Christian worldview, while other authors using the same title do not.)

Losing You Too Soon (previously titled *A Deeper Shade of Grace*) by Bernadette Keaggy
Biography of Christian music artist Phil Keaggy and his wife, Bernadette, relating their struggle through the deaths of five babies, including a set of triplets.

Misty by Carole Gift Page
Personal story of pregnancy complication and infant death.

Forever in Our Hearts by Russ and June Gordon
A high-quality photo journal for those who have experienced pregnancy loss or early infant death.
www.quietrefuge.com

I'll Hold You in Heaven Remembrance Book by Debbie Heydrick
Stories, prayers, and journaling pages for personal remembrance.

Morning Will Come and *The Memories I Cherish*, Caleb Ministries
> A collection of personal stories dealing with infertility, pregnancy loss, and infant death, and a keepsake journal for processing loss.
> www.calebministries.org/calebcares

*The Toughest Days of Grief** by Meg Woodson
> General grief book addressing specific landmark dates such holidays, birthdays, and anniversaries.

Mommies Enduring Neonatal Death (M.E.N.D.)
> Christian outreach to those who have lost a child due to miscarriage, stillbirth, or early infant death. Support groups, quarterly newsletter, and website.
> www.mend.org

A Place to Remember
> Resources for problem pregnancy, grief, and loss, including several items useful in planning funerals or memorial services after miscarriage, stillbirth, and infant death. (Not specifically a Christian resource.)
> www.aplacetoremember.com

Post-abortion

Tilly by Frank E. Peretti
> Fictional story of grace and forgiveness.

God's Grace
> Resources for post-abortive women now facing infertility and/or pregnancy loss.
> www.hannah.org/ministries/grace.htm

Living in His Forgiveness by Sandy Day with Carolyn McGuire
www.calebministries.org/abbeysplace

Adoption Loss

Nathaniel's Law
Families struggling through custody battles.
www.babynate.org

Adoption

Shaohannah's Hope
Founded by Steven Curtis Chapman and wife, Mary Beth, to care for orphans by engaging the church and helping Christian families reduce the financial barrier to adoption.
www.shaohannahshope.org

Snowflakes
Christian embryo adoption program.
www.snowflakes.org

Pregnancy and Parenting

Course of Time
Adoption/pregnancy after infertility, subsequent pregnancy after loss, and parenthood.
www.hannah.org/resources/cot.htm

Sidelines
Support for women and their families experiencing complicated pregnancy where the life or health of the mother or baby may be at

risk. (Not specifically a Christian resource.)
www.sidelines.org

Christian Living

Books by Janette Oke, Christian romance author
Infertility, miscarriage, stillbirth, infant death, and adoption loss
are common themes woven through many of this author's fiction
stories set in prairie times. The Canadian West series and *A Bride for
Donnigan* are wonderful examples.
www.janetteoke.com

"Wait" by Russell Kelfer
www.waitpoem.com and www.dtm.org

A Graceful Waiting* by Jan Frank
Best book I've ever read on the topic of waiting.
www.janfrank.org

Today's Christian Woman magazine
Practical, biblical advice for today's Christian woman.
www.TodaysChristianWoman.com

Women of Faith
Conferences, books, website, and more.
www.womenoffaith.com

Focus on the Family
Christian resources for all stages of family life.
www.family.org

Family Life Today
>   Marriage and family ministry.
>   www.fltoday.com

Rest Ministries
>   Christian support for chronic pain and illness. Support groups, *Hope
>   Keepers* magazine, e-mail devotionals, online community.
>   www.restministries.org

Music

"Thought You'd Be Here" by Wes King
>   From the album *Room Full of Stories.* Christian music artist shares his
>   reflections on infertility.
>   www.wesking.com

"Glory Baby" by Watermark
>   Song for baby miscarried, stillborn, or died in infancy. Look for *All
>   Things New* album.
>   www.watermark-online.com

"Visitor from Heaven" by Twila Paris
>   Saying good-bye to a child.
>   www.twilaparis.com

"Goodbye For Now" and "A Baby's Prayer" by Kathy Troccoli
>   The first is a mother's good-bye to her child. The second is an aborted
>   baby's prayer of comfort for her mother.
>   www.troccoli.com

"Home Free" by Wayne Watson
> The hope of heaven after the death of a loved one.
> www.waynewatson.com

"When Love Takes You In" by Steven Curtis Chapman
> Song written by adoptive dad, comparing human adoption to God's
> adoptive love for us.
> www.stevencurtischapman.com

"They Called Him Laughter" and "Joseph's Song" by Michael Card
> Reflections on the birth of Isaac in Abraham and Sarah's old age. And a
> song sharing Joseph's feelings as Jesus' adoptive father.
> www.michaelcard.com

> *No longer in print, but can typically be found through used book
> resources or libraries.*

seminal collection devices

In chapter 4, I referred to a special condom for sperm collection called a seminal collection device, or SCD. Made from sterile, medical-grade materials without any spermicidal properties, this condom can be used to collect for analysis and is only available by prescription. (Brand names and distributor information are easily found through Internet searches.) Once collected, the sample can be put into a small test tube, slipped into the wife's bra (for temperature control), and transported to a lab.

If you have male factor issues, manual collection may compound problems. Studies show that samples collected through SCDs and intercourse consistently come back with higher counts and quality than those collected through masturbation. While your doctor should have easy access to SCDs, surprisingly many doctors do not offer this option; you may need to specifically ask for such information.

While SCDs work very well for many, a few couples have shared that SCDs actually made collection more stressful for them. Because they are not lubricated, these condoms are difficult for some to use. One woman reported the condoms to be such a tight fit for her husband that he was unable to produce any sample due to discomfort. If the first brand you try doesn't work, look for others. If you ultimately find they just won't work for you, keep seeking the Lord's direction until He leads you to the right answer.

reproductive terms

This is not meant to be a comprehensive explanation of medical techniques available to achieve conception. Appendix A (Resources) lists several sources of information. I just want to give a brief description of some common methods we considered and which I discussed in this book.

adoption: To fully accept as your own, a child to whom you have no genetic relationship. To become the legal guardian and/or emotional parent of a child.

Assisted Reproductive Technologies (ARTs): A collection of medical procedures used to assist reproduction, such as *IUI* or *IVF*.

biological mother: The relationship a woman has to the baby carried in her womb.

chemical pregnancy: An early pregnancy, confirmed only by chemical methods (urine or blood test) but not by ultrasound.

Clomid: A common brand name for "clomiphene citrate," an oral medication prescribed to induce ovulation.

conception: The formation of a new entity of the same species as its parents, also referred to as *fertilization*. In human conception it can be presumed that the union of egg and sperm signify the immediate creation of a new soul, capable of fellowship with God.

cryo-preservation: The storage of eggs, sperm, or embryos in a frozen state, using liquid nitrogen.

ectopic pregnancy: A pregnancy in which the baby implants somewhere other than the mother's uterus, often in a fallopian tube. The mother's life is usually at risk as the pregnancy progresses.

embryo: A medical term to categorize the development of a baby from fertilization through the eighth week of pregnancy.

embryo adoption/donation: The transfer of an embryo into the uterus of a woman who plans to parent this child, though she has no genetic connection to baby. The *adoptive mother* becomes the baby's *biological mother* through the process of pregnancy. *Genetic parents* may choose to relinquish their embryos for adoption (rather than allowing the tragic alternatives of abandonment, scientific experimentation, or destruction) if they are medically unable to attempt future pregnancy or if they have remaining frozen embryos after building their families to desired size. *Donation* is viewed primarily as a medical procedure and handled directly through fertility clinics and lawyers. *Adoption* is facilitated through an adoption agency, typically allowing more involvement from the genetic family and requiring a home study for the adoptive family.

embryo transfer: The placement of an embryo fertilized in the laboratory, into a woman's uterus.

endometriosis: A disease characterized by the growth of endometrium (tissue lining the uterus) outside of the uterus, causing lesions which may respond to the hormones of a woman's menstrual cycle by causing bleeding, inflammation, pain, adhesions, scar tissue, and infertility. Symptoms may include intense cramping and pain prior to and during menstruation, pain with intercourse, painful urination or bowel movements, diarrhea, constipation, and nausea.

fallopian tubes: Thin tubes that provide a passageway for eggs to travel from ovaries to the uterus.

fetus: A Latin word simply meaning, "little one," this is the technical term for a developing baby from nine weeks after fertilization until birth.

follicle: A "cyst" containing a maturing egg. When the follicle ruptures to release an egg from the ovary, the process is called *ovulation.*

follicle reduction: Used in conjunction with IUI, this is the medical retrieval and destruction (without exposure to sperm) of excess eggs, prior to ovulation, in an attempt to prevent the conception of more babies than a mother can safely carry in a single pregnancy.

follicle-stimulating hormone (FSH): A hormone of the pituitary gland that stimulates the growth of follicles in the ovary or sperm within the testes. Can be given by injection during ARTS procedures to induce ovulation.

gametes: Eggs or sperm.

genetic parent: The man or woman who provides the egg or sperm used in the conception of a child.

gonadotropins: Hormones that stimulate egg production by the ovaries and sperm production by the testicles. LH and FSH are *gonadotropins.*

home study: A process intended to educate and prepare families for adoption while allowing social workers to evaluate the fitness of the adoptive family to meet the needs of specific children they may be matched with. Legal requirements vary greatly from state to state and country to country.

human chorionic gonadotropin (hCG): The "pregnancy hormone" detectable via urine or blood testing. A woman's blood test is typically considered "positive" for pregnancy if hCG levels are at least 10 mIU/mL. This number rises rapidly during the early weeks of a healthy pregnancy. HCG is sometimes administered by injection to trigger ovulation in ARTs procedures. (Taking a pregnancy test too soon after hCG injection can cause a "false positive" pregnancy reading.)

hysterosalpingogram (HSG): A procedure where x-ray observation of a woman's uterus and fallopian tubes is conducted by injecting dye through the cervix, allowing medical staff to evaluate uterine shape and patency (openness) of tubes.

implantation: The burrowing of an embryo into its mother's uterine lining.

infertility: The inability to conceive within one year (six months if a woman is over age 35) of regular sexual relations without the use of birth control methods, or the inability to carry a child to live birth. The nature of *infertility* can be either *primary* (thus no living children) or *secondary* (facing fertility challenges after having given live birth at least once).

intrauterine insemination (IUI): A medical process for placing washed sperm into a woman's uterus near the time of ovulation. If using the sperm of a woman's own husband, this process can be called *Artificial Insemination by Husband (AIH)*. When a sperm donor is used, the procedure is called *Artificial Insemination by Donor (AID)* or *Donor Insemination (DI)*.

In vitro fertilization (IVF): Eggs and sperm are collected from each partner and placed together to incubate outside the woman's body. If eggs are fertilized, developing embryos are then transferred into the mother's uterus and/or frozen for future pregnancy attempts.

laparoscopy: "Band-Aid surgery" where a narrow telescope (*laparoscope*) is inserted through small incisions in a woman's abdomen for the purpose of examining the exterior of her reproductive organs. Conditions such as *endometriosis* and adhesions can often be diagnosed via laparoscopic procedure. While relatively minor, this process can still be rather painful and require several days of recovery.

laparotomy: A major surgery, performed under direct vision, requiring open incision of the abdomen.

luteal phase: The time between a woman's ovulation and the beginning of her next menstrual period, typically about fourteen days.

luteal phase defect (LPD): A common cause of early miscarriage due to low progesterone levels and a shortened second half of a woman's menstrual cycle.

luteinizing hormone (LH): A hormone of the pituitary gland that causes a woman's ovary to release a mature egg or to stimulate testosterone production in men.

miscarriage: The death of a baby prior to twenty weeks gestation.

ovaries: Female reproductive organs that produce the hormones estrogen and progesterone. Eggs are formed in ovarian *follicles*, then released in the act of *ovulation*.

ovulate: To release one or more eggs from an ovary.

selective reduction: The intentional abortion of one of more babies in a multiple pregnancy.

sperm washing: The separation of sperm from seminal fluids.

sterility: Permanent inability to produce the genetic materials needed for conception, or the lack of a woman's uterus.

stillbirth: The death of a baby in its mother's womb, after twenty weeks gestational age and up to the moment of delivery.

Sudden Infant Death Syndrome (SIDS): The sudden and unexplained death of an infant who is younger than one year of age.

superovulation: The use of fertility drugs to stimulate a woman's ovaries to develop more than one egg.

ultrasound: The use of sound waves to produce an image used to evaluate pregnancy or ovarian activity.

uterus: A woman's reproductive organ, sometimes called the *womb*, designed to facilitate the nourishment and growth of a baby from the point of *implantation* until birth.

notes

Chapter 1: Family Ties

1. Debra Bridwell, *The Ache for a Child* (Wheaton, Ill.: Victor, 1994), p. 27.

Chapter 4: Because He Loved Her

1. Rabbi Michael Gold, *And Hannah Wept* (Philadelphia, New York, Jerusalem: The Jewish Publication Society, 1988), pp. 47-48.

Chapter 5: Put Yourself in My Shoes
(Before You Put Your Foot in Your Mouth)

1. Ginger Garrett, *Moments for Couples Who Long for Children* (Colorado Springs, Colo.: NavPress, 2003), p. 27.

Chapter 7: Two Hearts Beating as One . . . Sometimes

1. Michele Weiner-Davis Training Corp., copyright 2004 Reprinted with permission of Michele Weiner-Davis, author of *The Sex-Starved Marriage* and Developer of divorcebusting.com.

Chapter 11: Prayer, Faith, and Compassion

1. Bruce Wilkinson, *The Prayer of Jabez* (Sisters, Ore.: Multnomah, 2000), p. 24.
2. Wilkinson, p. 24.

Chapter 13: Anguish and Grief

1. Beth Moore, *Feathers from My Nest* (Nashville, Tenn.: Broadman & Holman, 2001), pp. 30-31.
2. Beth Moore, *Things Pondered* (Nashville, Tenn.: Broadman & Holman, 2004), p. 55.

Chapter 15: Worshiping While Waiting

1. *Matthew Henry's Commentary* (1710), public domain.
2. Bruce Wilkinson, *The Prayer of Jabez* (Sisters, Ore.: Multnomah, 2000), p. 23.

3. Jan Frank, *A Graceful Waiting* (Ann Arbor, Mich.: Vine Books, 1996), p. 188.

4. Jennifer Saake, copyright 1994.

5. "Wait" taken from *Follow Me!* by Russell Kelfer, copyright 1995. Published by Discipleship Tape Ministries, Inc., and Into His Likeness Publications. Used by permission.

6. Ginger Garrett, *Moments for Couples Who Long for Children* (Colorado Springs, Colo.: NavPress, 2003), pp. 39-40.

Chapter 16: In the Course of Time

1. *Webster's Ninth New Collegiate Dictionary*, s.v. "Mother."

2. John MacArthur, *Safe in the Arms of God* (Nashville, Tenn.: Thomas Nelson, 2003), p. 147.

3. MacArthur, p. 68.

4. Judy Gann, "A Spiritual Mom," *Woman's Touch*, May/June 2004, p. 22. Used by permission.

Epilogue

1. Jan Frank, *A Graceful Waiting* (Ann Arbor, Mich.: Vine Books, 1996), p. 40.

about the author

It is not by coincidence that God has allowed you to find this book. He has known you by name since before I even dreamed of writing. With each word typed, I've prayed that He would minister to your needs. Thank you for allowing Hannah and me the great privilege of sharing your heart's journey.

Love, Jenni

Jennifer Saake (pronounced *say-key*) was born in 1972, the second living child of Ralph and Betty Camp after their battle through secondary infertility. Her childhood years were spent on the mission field, primarily in Japan.

Rick entered her life in 1990, while both were students at The Master's College in Southern California. In spite of her struggle with Chronic Fatigue Immune Dysfunction Syndrome, they married in August 1992. They planned to build a large family through both birth and adoption.

God's plans instead led them to birth Hannah's Prayer Ministries, a Christ-centered support ministry for families facing fertility challenges, including infertility, pregnancy loss, and early infant death. Jennifer is director emeritus of this organization.

The Saakes make their home in northern Nevada, where they enjoy bike riding, gardening, and visiting Lake Tahoe with their two living children. Jennifer is thankful for the privilege of being a stay-at-home mom and homeschool teacher. Her freelance writing has led to prolific publication in infertility and bereavement periodicals, along with pieces in a few mainstream magazines and devotional books.

Visit Jenni at www.jennifer.saake.biz.

LEARN TO TURN YOUR FOCUS ON GOD, NOT ON YOUR CIRCUMSTANCES

The Blessing Book

Linda Dillow   1-57683-464-6

When we find ourselves in the valley, we must remember to turn our eyes off the suffering and onto the Healer—He can make it a place of blessing.

Tame Your Fears

Carol Kent   1-57683-359-3

Carol Kent suggests ways to overcome your fears by using them as stepping stones to deeper faith, renewed confidence, and sincere reverence for a powerful and loving God.

On Broken Legs

Wendy Murray Zoba   1-57683-643-6

This beautifully written literary memoir shows us how God uses personal crises to both shatter and rebuild our faith.

To order copies, visit your local Christian bookstore,
call NavPress at 1-800-366-7788, or log on to www.navpress.com.

To locate a Christian bookstore near you,
call 1-800-991-7747.

NAVPRESS

BRINGING TRUTH TO LIFE
www.navpress.com